Nick Stellino's
Family Kitchen

G. P. PUTNAM'S SONS
NEW YORK

Nick Stellino's

Family Kitchen

PHOTOGRAPHS BY E. J. ARMSTRONG

G. P. Putnam's Sons
Publishers Since 1838
a member of
Penguin Putnam Inc.
375 Hudson Street
New York, NY 10014

Library of Congress Cataloging-in-Publication Data

Stellino, Nick.
  [Family kitchen]
  Nick Stellino's family kitchen / photographs by
E. J. Armstrong.
    p. cm.
  ISBN 0-399-14533-8
  1. Cookery, Italian. 2. Menus. I. Title.
II. Title: Family kitchen.
TX723.S7955   1999   99-15967 CIP
641.5945–dc21

Printed in the United States of America
10 9 8 7 6 5 4 3 2 1

This book is printed on acid-free paper. ∞

BOOK DESIGN BY DEBORAH KERNER

This book is dedicated to everyone

who dares to dream.

All successes are based on

a foundation of failures.

But with the steadfast support

of passion,

enthusiasm, and

determination,

any dream is bound

to become a reality.

Never let go of your dreams,

for they are the breath of life.

Acknowledgments

The making of this book has been a very special event in my life. This is the first project that my wife, Nanci, and I have produced together. Nanci deserves a medal for her patience and understanding. There were plenty of times when I became discouraged, yet she always helped me recharge my ambition.

I particularly thank my editor, John Duff, for his gentle editing, and more important, for once again giving me the opportunity to tell my stories.

The photographs in the book are the masterly work of my good friend E. J. Armstrong. The food was styled with consummate grace, by Patty Wittman. I am grateful to them, and to the wonderful team of dedicated culinary artists who collaborated with me in testing the recipes: Susan Volland, Deb Winson, and Denise Vivaldo.

Finally, I thank my family for their constant belief and support: my mother Massimiliana, my father Vincenzo, my brother Mario; my aunt Buliti, my uncle Michele, my cousins Veronica and Gerri; my uncle Franz, my aunt Titi, my cousins Attila and Tiziana; my in-laws Sol and Gitte, Toby, and Alan; and my nephews Josh and Andrew.

Contents

All Together in the Family Kitchen

Whenever I am asked why Americans love Italian food so much, my first response is, "Because it tastes great!" But the real answer, the one I feel respects the traditions of generations of Italian cooks, goes much deeper.

If I think of my own family's connection with food, I am flooded with memories, vivid images of smiling faces, familiar voices, and music. Most of all, though, it is smells and tastes that carry me back to the hours spent around my family's dinner table in our modest home in Palermo, Sicily.

Every time I visit my family, I rediscover the important role food and wine play in the daily lives of all Italians. Food holds our culture together. It animates our daily chores. Visits to open markets teach us not only about good, fresh ingredients, but also about the subtle art of personal relations, joyful negotiations, buying and selling. Here we are engaged with the merchants who, for generations, have been the first link in the chain that connects us to the bounty of Mother Nature. From the sweetest tomato to the freshest fish to the juiciest of cured olives spilling out of handmade baskets.

Even in the midst of what might appear to the casual observer nothing but chaos, a certain ritual is played out day after day in these marketplaces. When I go to the market, my father in the lead, we start by selecting vegetables, then bread, cheese, and finally the meat and fish. With his childlike enthusiasm—which has remained undiminished to this day—my father moves nimbly from stand to stand, scrutinizing the offerings, aggressively negotiating prices. With each selection, he adds a new element to what will be the family dinner—a slash of red, a burst of yellow, a blossom of green.

When Italians talk about food, they are talking about their souls. Our culinary traditions are the sacred thread that runs through the tapestry of our lives.

Our sense of family and community is so intertwined with the rituals of shopping and preparing, of eating and drinking, that these activities virtually define our past, describe our present, and shape our future.

All this over a plate of pasta with some tomato sauce?

When I cook, no matter how simple or sophisticated the recipe, I move through a series of steps that are part of a ritual that has taken place almost unchanged for many generations. As I set out the ingredients, I sing (rather poorly, I must admit) one of my uncle Giovanni's favorite arias. And I consider each ingredient like a note which, when properly assembled and orchestrated with others, creates a passionate song.

Even as I slice garlic and chop onions, I sense Nonna Adele's gentle caress on the back of my head. I feel her presence near me. For it was under her guidance that I first experienced the joy of cooking. I am transported back to my grandma's small kitchen in a rural town in Sicily. . . .

I am standing next to her, on a wooden stool by the stove. Garlic and onions sizzle in the oil in the pot. With big breaths I inhale the seductive aromas whirling around us. Nonna Adele guides my unsteady hand, and together, we stir the ingredients with a long-handled wooden spoon. I feel like a grand *monzù* (Sicilian master chef). I look up at her wrinkled face. Her soulful eyes light up, and her lips open in a loving smile. *"Bravo,"* she says. *"Bravo, Nicolino."* And I feel proud.

My father, Vincenzo, sits at the end of a long wooden table grating the Parmesan, coaxing every nuance of flavor from the hard block of cheese. My aunt Buliti and my mother, Massimiliana, are talking vivaciously, laughing and gossiping like teenagers. Meanwhile their nimble fingers peel fresh-picked garden tomatoes.

"Vacci piano," warns my father. *"Fa' attenzione, non l'ammaccare."* Be careful. Pay attention, don't bruise them. My mother looks over to him, rolling her eyes: *"Gratta il formaggio, tu, al resto ci penso io!"* You grate the cheese, I'll take care of the rest!

Meanwhile, Mario, my brother, sitting in the high chair next to my father, unobserved sticks his little hand into the bowl of grated cheese and with a single swift movement shoves a fistful into his mouth.

"Guarda, un altro buongustaio"–Look, another gourmand has joined the ranks–Nonna Adele says, a ripple of laughter in her voice. As my father wipes Mario's hands, we all join in laughing, captivated by the moment.

From the next room, the haunting melody of a Puccini aria echoes from an old record player. My uncle Giovanni sings along in his soft voice, probably sitting hunched close to the speaker, his hand moving rhythmically, deftly, directing the orchestra. Only the scents rising from the kitchen will draw him away from his music.

Finally, the preparations are ended, the table is set, and the family gathers around the table. My father uncorks the wine. Then comes the food. It is laid out along the table, beautiful, inviting, and comforting. We raise our glasses. *"Cent'anni!"* May we all live to be a hundred! *"Buon appetito!"*

As the music plays on in my memory and the aromas from the past surround me, I return to the present. Here in my own kitchen I feel the presence of those loved ones so intensely that I can't help looking around to see if they are here, waiting expectantly for the meal to be served. The memories of the times we spent together around the dinner table are more precious than gold to me. There we shared our joys and our sorrows, and great food and wine–the ingredients for the celebration of life.

With this book, inspired by the traditions of my own family, I hope that you too can rediscover the joys of the family kitchen. I have tried to make the recipes and menus simple and versatile so that they can become a part of your family traditions. Please join me and my family–those special people who live forever in my heart–on this culinary adventure.

Her Name Was Mariuccia

It was July 1975, a few weeks before I was to leave for America. My father and I were heading home after shopping for lunch at the Vucciria, the oldest open market in Palermo. Our car was loaded down with a selection of wonderful fresh food, and the aroma of garlic, fresh vegetables, cheeses, and salamis teased our appetites: another memorable meal in the Stellino kitchen was promised.

Throughout our buying spree, my father had been unusually quiet and reserved. Even bargaining with the food vendors, his favorite activity, had not made him more talkative. As we were driving home, barely a word between us, he took an unexpected turn toward the harbor. I looked at him, but he didn't look back at me. Maybe he wanted to make one last stop at Don Gioacchino's fishery, I thought, one of his regular haunts in that part of town. Instead he drove the car past the harbor gates and parked on a farther pier. I had been there once before, when we had taken a boat to Naples.

He got out of the car and walked slowly along the pier. I followed, thinking he wanted to show me something. At the end of the pier, he stopped and gazed out toward the brilliant blue Mediterranean. In silent anticipation, I stood beside him as the summer breeze blew softly against our faces. Before us, a multitude of colorful fishing boats clustered together, as cargo ships moved slowly in the distance. He lit a cigarette, covering the flame from the breeze, then took a long, deep drag, and murmured, "Her name was Mariuccia." He took another drag. The smoke blew out of his nostrils in a thick cloud, as he stared ahead.

Who was Mariuccia? I asked myself. I had been so preoccupied preparing for my departure, which would take me away from my father for months or years, that strange thoughts raced around my head. I looked into his face, anxious for some explanation.

He said it again: "Her name was Mariuccia." As he spoke, he reached inside his pocket and pulled out a piece of paper, yellowed with age. Without a word he handed it to me, gesturing subtly that I should open it. I took the paper from his hand and unfolded it carefully so that I would not tear it along the folds.

The first thing that caught my attention was the date, January 1958—four months before I was born. I glanced at him before I continued. His eyes were moist and his lips pursed; clearly, he was holding back some deep emotion. I read on, line by line. This was an emigration certificate for Mr. and Mrs. Vincenzo Stellino. Departure: January 1958, from Palermo. Destination: New York. The name of the ship that would have taken my mother and father to America was still legible on the fading document: *Mariuccia.*

Now, for the first time, I understood what my father meant whenever he told my younger brother and me, *"L'America è un sogno!"* America is a dream! The dream that one day had been his was now soon to be mine.

Fighting back my own tears, I kissed him on one cheek and whispered, *"Papà, ti voglio bene."* Dad, I love you. I held his hand, and together we stood at the end of the pier, staring out at the horizon, dreaming of a land on the other side of the world.

After a few moments of reverie, my father ran his hand over my head, the way he used to do when I was a kid. *"Nicolino, hai fame?"* he asked.

I nodded: yes, I was hungry. He pinched my cheeks with both hands, and with a big smile said, "Let's go home and cook. There is a special dish I want to teach you. Maybe one day you will prepare it for your friends in America. Remember, Nicolino, *l'America è un sogno!"*

Appetizers

Toasted Bread with Onion and Pancetta

Baked Eggs with Spinach and Ricotta

Baked Zucchini Stuffed with Salami

Braised Artichokes

Little Bruschette

Shrimp Fritters with Roasted Garlic Sauce

Little Pizzas

Stuffed Peppers with Tomatoes, Mozzarella,

Capers, and Olives

Rollatini

Sautéed Calamari with Sun-Dried Tomatoes

Scallops on a Bed of Leeks and Artichokes

Scallops with Prosciutto and Morels

Fried Shrimp with Pine Nuts and Herbs

Trio of Stuffed Eggs

Mushroom and Crêpe Torte

Stuffed Calamari

Truffled Breadsticks

Toasted Bread with Onion and Pancetta

CIPUDDATA

SERVES 6

12 ¾-inch-thick slices day-old round or oval country bread, about 3 to 4
    inches in diameter
2 whole cloves garlic, plus 3 cloves thickly sliced
3 tablespoons plus ¼ cup olive oil
¼ teaspoon red pepper flakes
8 ounces pancetta or bacon, sliced ¼ inch thick, roughly chopped
½ medium white onion, thinly sliced
1 35-ounce can Italian-style tomatoes, drained, coarsely chopped,
    juice reserved (or use stewed tomatoes for a slightly sweeter taste)
2 heaping tablespoons chopped fresh basil
3 tablespoons chopped fresh parsley
⅛ teaspoon dry oregano
Salt to taste
12 teaspoons (¼ cup) freshly grated Romano cheese

My grandma always found a way to use leftovers and magically turn them into the most delicious dishes. The aroma and smoky flavor of these little treats will leave everyone begging for more. The word cipuddata *comes from the Sicilian for "onion."*

Preheat oven broiler.

Place the slices of bread on a sheet pan. Toast in the oven, on both sides. Rub one side of each slice of toast with the 2 whole garlic cloves.

In a deep, wide sauté pan, heat the 3 tablespoons olive oil over medium heat. Add the red pepper flakes, sliced garlic, pancetta, and onion. Cook for 6 to 9 minutes, until the onion is soft and it and the garlic just begin to brown. Add the tomatoes, basil, parsley, and oregano, and cook until the tomatoes have lost most of their water, about 3 to 4 minutes. Add 1 cup of the reserved tomato juice. Bring to a boil, reduce heat, and simmer for 4 to 5 minutes. The mixture will be like a thick and chunky salsa. Taste for salt, and season if desired.

When the mixture is ready, spoon it on top of the slices of toast. Drizzle the ¼ cup olive oil evenly over the top, and sprinkle each piece of toast with 1 teaspoon of the cheese. Broil in the oven for 2 minutes, until the cheese is melted, making sure not to burn the bread.

Serve 2 pieces per person, accompanied by a green salad.

Baked Eggs with Spinach and Ricotta

UOVA PASQUALINE

SERVES 6

10 large eggs at room temperature (6 for boiling, 2 for filling, 2 for wash)
2 to 4 tablespoons olive oil
8 ounces honey-baked ham, cut into ¼-inch dice
1¼ pounds (2 10-ounce bags) spinach, washed, rinsed, and dried, thick stems removed
Salt and pepper to taste
8 ounces ricotta cheese
½ cup Italian-Style Bread Crumbs (see page 230)
1 cup freshly grated Romano cheese
Flour for working pastry dough
2 9½x10-inch sheets frozen puff pastry, thawed
1 recipe Creamed Tomato Sauce (see page 237)
2 tablespoons chopped fresh parsley

This is a very simple dish that, as my wife says, is quite cute. It was a favorite of my brother's and mine around Eastertime.

Preheat oven to 375°. Line a sheet tray with parchment paper.

Place 6 of the eggs in a pot of cold water. Bring to a boil. Reduce heat and simmer for 10 minutes. Drain well and set aside to cool. Peel when cool enough to handle.

In a deep, wide sauté pan, heat 2 tablespoons of the olive oil over medium heat. Add the ham and sauté for 2 minutes over medium-high heat. Add the spinach and sauté until wilted, about 2 to 3 minutes; you may have to cook it in batches, adding oil if necessary. Season with salt and pepper. Cook 2 more minutes, until the spinach is fairly dry. Remove the mixture and chop finely.

In a deep bowl, combine the spinach mixture with the ricotta, 2 uncooked eggs, bread crumbs, and Romano cheese. The mixture should be thick, not runny, and should hold together.

Prepare the egg wash by whisking together the remaining 2 uncooked eggs with 2 teaspoons water.

On a lightly floured surface, lay out a pastry sheet (keep the other wrapped in the refrigerator until ready to use). Roll to about an 11x11-inch square, and cut into four 5-½ inch squares. Roll each piece further, to 6-inch squares. Roll everything out quickly; you don't want to give the butter in the dough a chance to melt, or you'll end up with chewy rather than flaky pastry. As you roll out the pastry dough, dust as necessary with additional flour, to prevent its sticking to the surface or rolling pin. Dust off all excess flour before filling the pastry. Follow the same procedure with the second piece of dough. (You need only 6 squares total; you may wrap and refreeze excess pieces for future use.)

Coat each hard-boiled egg with a sixth of the spinach mixture. Brush the inside edges of the pastry squares generously with the wash. Place each coated egg in the center of a pastry square, and pull the four corners up to meet in the center above the egg. Seal the seams by pinching them together, and make sure there are no exposed bits of filling. The pastry will cooperate; do not overwork or overhandle.

Place the egg pouches on the prepared sheet tray. Brush the tops with the remaining egg wash. Bake for about 20 minutes, or until golden brown.

While the pouches are baking, make the tomato sauce. Spoon the sauce in the bottom of 6 dishes. When the pouches are done, place one on each dish. Sprinkle with the parsley.

Baked Zucchini Stuffed with Salami

ZUCCHINE RIPIENE AL FORNO

SERVES 6 GENEROUSLY

6 small zucchini
4 tablespoons olive oil
1 cup chopped onion
8 ounces salami, chopped
½ cup pine nuts
¼ cup chopped fresh basil
6 cloves garlic, thickly sliced
½ teaspoon salt
½ teaspoon freshly ground black pepper
¼ teaspoon red pepper flakes
1 cup white wine
½ cup Italian-Style Bread Crumbs (see page 230)
¾ cup freshly grated Romano cheese
Salt and pepper to taste
1 recipe Spicy Tomato Sauce (see page 238)

This recipe is especially suited for people who think vegetables are boring. It's a hearty dish that will have even the most finicky eater asking for more.

Preheat oven to 400°.

Trim the ends of the zucchini, and blanch the zucchini whole in boiling water for 4 minutes. Slice in half lengthwise. With a pear corer, melon-ball knife, or small spoon, scoop out the insides, leaving a ¼-inch-thick shell or "boat." Chop the scooped-out pulp.

In a large sauté pan, heat the olive oil over medium heat. Add the chopped zucchini pulp, onion, salami, pine nuts, basil, garlic, salt, pepper, and red pepper flakes, and cook until the onion is tender and the pine nuts begin to brown, about 10 to 12 minutes. Stir in the wine and simmer until liquid is reduced by half, about 2 to 3 minutes. Remove from heat and cool slightly. Combine the mixture with the bread crumbs and ½ cup of the cheese to make a moist stuffing.

Sprinkle the zucchini boats with a little salt and pepper. Spoon ½ cup of the stuffing into each of the boats and place them on a lightly greased baking pan. Sprinkle with the remaining cheese. Bake until the cheese is brown and the filling is cooked through, 20 to 25 minutes.

While the zucchini are baking, make the tomato sauce. Serve the sauce alongside the stuffed zucchini.

Braised Artichokes

CARCIOFI BRASATI

SERVES 6

6 tablespoons olive oil
1 medium white onion, thinly sliced
8 cloves garlic, thickly sliced
¼ teaspoon red pepper flakes
¼ teaspoon dry thyme
6 fresh artichokes, cleaned and quartered (see tip below)
1 cup white wine
2 cups Chicken Stock (see page 231) or canned vegetable stock
2 tablespoons chopped fresh parsley
Salt and pepper to taste

Surprise your guests with this robust, rustic-looking dish, a great accompaniment to an entree or a perfect meal by itself. Make sure you have plenty of Italian bread to dip into the tasty sauce.

In a wide saucepan or a 12-inch skillet, heat the olive oil over medium heat. Add the onion, garlic, red pepper flakes, and thyme. Cook for 15 minutes, stirring every 5 minutes until the onion and garlic start to brown.

Increase heat to high, add the artichokes, and cook, stirring well, for 3 to 5 minutes. Add the wine and cook for 3 to 5 minutes, until liquid is reduced by half, stirring well to dislodge any browned bits at the bottom of the pan. Add the stock and bring to a boil. Add the parsley, stir well, and reduce heat to simmer. Almost cover the pan, and simmer for 25 to 30 minutes.

Add salt and pepper to taste. Serve with fresh Italian bread.

Chef's Tip

How to clean and quarter a fresh artichoke

Squeeze the juice of a lemon into a large bowl of cold water. Rub your hands with the lemon rinds to prevent your skin from being stained. Pull back the first few layers of tough outer leaves of the artichoke by bending them back, one at a time, until they snap off. Turn the artichoke upside down and hold it like an ice cream cone—be careful of the thorns. With a sharp paring knife, cut away the dark green part at the bottom now facing you; use the same clockwise motion you would use to peel an apple.

Now get rid of the leaves with spiny thorns at the top. Hold the artichoke flat on a cutting board, and with the point of a sharp chef's knife, cut a hole across the width of the leaves about 2 to 2½ inches from the bottom. This will make it easy to slice off the thorny part of the leaves. They may be resistant, and sometimes it is difficult to cut across in a single motion, even with a sharp knife. Place the knife blade into the hole, slice off the tops of the leaves, and cut the artichoke in quarters.

Hold a quartered piece flat on the cutting board, cut side facing you, and put the point of the knife behind the last row of purple leaves encasing the hairy choke. With a slow and steady motion, cut off the core. Be careful not to slice off the tender flesh of the heart. Concentrate on the leaves, and cut them off at the base where they are attached to the bottom. Place the quartered pieces in the bowl filled with cold water until ready to use.

Little Bruschelle

BRUSCHETTINE

SERVES 6 TO 8

8 Roma (pear) tomatoes, seeded and finely diced
3 cloves garlic, finely chopped, plus 3 whole cloves
5 tablespoons extra-virgin olive oil
2 tablespoons balsamic vinegar
3 tablespoons finely chopped fresh basil
¾ teaspoon salt
½ teaspoon freshly ground black pepper
1 baguette, 2½ to 3 inches in diameter, cut in 20 ¼-inch slices

Preheat oven broiler.

In a large bowl, stir together the tomatoes, chopped garlic, olive oil, vinegar, basil, salt, and pepper until well mixed. Let rest at room temperature for 30 minutes.

Toast the bread slices on both sides under the broiler until well browned. When they are cool enough to handle, rub them on both sides with the whole garlic. Top each slice of toast with a heaping teaspoon of the tomato mixture. Place the bruschettine on a tray and serve.

Here is a fabulous rendition of a traditional recipe, ideal for serving at parties. The bruschettine are easy to make, taste great, and fit perfectly between thumb and forefinger.

Shrimp Fritters with Roasted Garlic Sauce

POLPETTINE DI GAMBERO AL SUGO D'AGLIO ARROSTITO

MAKES 18 TO 20 1½-INCH FRITTERS

1 pound medium shrimp, peeled, deveined, and roughly chopped

1 pound potatoes, peeled, boiled, and mashed (1½ cups mashed pulp)

1 cup freshly grated Parmesan cheese

1 egg, lightly beaten

1 tablespoon chopped fresh Italian parsley

1 teaspoon grated lemon zest

1 teaspoon salt

½ teaspoon freshly ground black pepper

½ cup Italian-Style Bread Crumbs (see page 230)

4 to 5 cups light or extra-light olive oil (see tip below)

1 recipe Roasted Garlic Sauce (see page 253)

Combine the shrimp, mashed potatoes, cheese, egg, parsley, lemon zest, salt, and pepper in a large bowl. Mix well with your hands or a wooden spoon until completely blended. Form into 1½-inch balls. Roll the balls in the bread crumbs. In a deep skillet, heat the olive oil over high heat, to 350° (little bubbles will form on the surface). Deep-fry the balls, only 4 or 5 at a time, for 2 to 3 minutes, until golden brown and cooked through. Add oil as needed, but be sure to keep the oil hot so

Even the most dignified dinner guest will find it hard to resist these little delicacies.

the shrimp do not absorb too much oil while cooking. Drain the fritters on crumpled paper towels, and keep warm. Serve with the Roasted Garlic Sauce.

Chef's Tip

Do not use extra-virgin or virgin olive oil for frying, as the oil will burn. "Extra-light" olive oil is preferable.

Little Pizzas

PIZZETTE

MAKES ENOUGH FINGER FOOD FOR A PARTY OF 10

These are a wonderful solution for the busy host or hostess who loves to entertain but does not have a lot of time to spend in the kitchen. With all the variations, you will have an abundance of delectable snacks to satisfy all your guests.

PIZZA BASE
6 9½x10-inch sheets frozen puff pastry, thawed
1 recipe Pizza Sauce (see page 242)
Salt and pepper to taste

MARGHERITA TOPPING
½ cup Pizza Sauce (see page 242)
8 ounces fresh mozzarella cheese, cut into ¼-inch dice
4 tablespoons chopped fresh basil
4 tablespoons freshly grated Parmesan cheese

PROSCIUTTO AND GORGONZOLA TOPPING
½ cup Pizza Sauce (see page 242)
¼ cup chopped prosciutto or ham (4 ounces)
¼ cup crumbled Gorgonzola cheese (4 ounces)
2 tablespoons chopped fresh Italian parsley
4 tablespoons freshly grated Parmesan cheese

TRUFFLED MUSHROOM TOPPING
2 cups cremini mushrooms, thinly sliced
½ cup Pizza Sauce (see page 242)
4 tablespoons chopped fresh Italian parsley
½ cup freshly grated Parmesan cheese
1 teaspoon truffle oil (1 drop for each pizzetta)

Preheat oven to 400°. Line 2 large baking sheets with aluminum foil or parchment paper.

Spread the Pizza Sauce evenly over the sheets of pastry, and cover evenly with the selected toppings. With a long, sharp knife cut each pastry sheet into 20 equal pieces, roughly 2 by 2½ inches. With a thin spatula transfer the pizzette onto the baking sheets. Bake 15 to 18 minutes, or until the pastry is brown and cooked through. Serve hot.

Chef's Tip

Hold back on the salt—there's plenty of flavor without it. For those who like that sodium kick, sprinkle salt lightly over the pizzette before baking. I would advise not to use more than ¼ teaspoon each of salt and pepper for the recipe.

Stuffed Peppers with Tomatoes, Mozzarella, Capers, and Olives

PEPERONI FARCITI ALLA PARTENOPEA

SERVES 6 GENEROUSLY

3 medium red bell peppers (see tip below)

3 medium yellow bell peppers (see tip below)

4 tablespoons olive oil

1 cup chopped onion

30 Kalamata or similar black olives, pitted and chopped

3 tablespoons drained capers

2 tablespoons chopped fresh Italian parsley

6 cloves garlic, thickly sliced

1 teaspoon anchovy paste

¼ teaspoon red pepper flakes

¼ teaspoon salt

½ teaspoon freshly ground black pepper

1 28-ounce can Italian-style stewed tomatoes, chopped, with juice

8 ounces fresh mozzarella cheese, cut into ½-inch cubes (1 cup)

½ cup Italian-Style Bread Crumbs (see page 230)

1 cup freshly grated Romano cheese

1 cup Tomato Sauce (see page 235)

1 cup Chicken Stock (see page 231)

My father fell in love with this recipe while he was stationed in Naples during his military service (the adjective partenopea *refers to Naples). From what he told me, he spent more time in the kitchen than in uniform. When I asked him why, he responded: "The only way to get a decent meal was to cook it myself!"*

Preheat oven to 400°.

Slice the peppers in half lengthwise. Scoop out the seeds and trim the stems and white membranes, and discard.

In a large saucepan, heat the olive oil over medium heat. Add the onion, olives, capers, parsley, garlic, anchovy paste, red pepper flakes, salt, and pepper, and sauté for 8 to 10 minutes, or until the onion is sweet and tender. Stir in the tomatoes with their packing juice and simmer for 8 to 10 minutes, or until the mixture is reduced to a light glaze. Remove from heat and cool slightly.

Pour the mixture into a large bowl, and combine with the mozzarella, bread crumbs, and ½ cup of the Romano cheese. This is the stuffing.

Mix the Tomato Sauce and Chicken Stock together and pour into a large baking dish. Spoon about ½ cup of the prepared stuffing into the pepper halves and arrange them over the sauce in the baking dish. Sprinkle the remaining Romano cheese over the peppers. Bake for 30 to 35 minutes, until the cheese is golden brown and the peppers are tender. Serve one red and one yellow pepper half per person with the sauce alongside.

Chef's Tip

For this recipe select smaller peppers; there won't be enough stuffing for big peppers, and they won't all fit in one baking pan. If you want the peppers to be any fuller, increase the amount of mozzarella. More bread crumbs make the stuffing too doughy.

Rollatini

ROLLATINI D'INSACCATI

SERVES 6

1 4-ounce jar sliced roasted red peppers, rinsed and well drained
1 clove garlic, finely chopped
1 teaspoon plus ¼ cup chopped fresh parsley
1 tablespoon olive oil
1 teaspoon balsamic vinegar
⅛ teaspoon salt
6 ounces prosciutto or ham, in 6 equal slices, thick enough for outer wrapping
4 ounces provolone cheese, cut in 12 very thin slices
4 ounces salami, cut in 12 very thin slices
4 ounces Swiss cheese, cut in 12 very thin slices
¼ red bell pepper, finely diced
Toothpicks (party or decorative picks if for a party)

*H*ere's another wonderful idea for your next party. The recipe is easy and quick to assemble, and will be a sure hit with everyone.

Combine the roasted peppers with the garlic, 1 teaspoon of the parsley, olive oil, vinegar, and salt. Toss well. Allow to marinate for at least 20 minutes.

On a piece of plastic wrap over a flat surface, lay out a slice of prosciutto from left to right in front of you. On top of it lay two slices of provolone, overlapping, if necessary, the length of the prosciutto. Follow in the same manner with the salami, then the Swiss cheese. Spoon about 2 teaspoons of the pepper marinade down the middle of the stack of meat and cheese (the length of the layered strip). Sprinkle with all but a teaspoon of the ¼ cup parsley.

Starting at the edge closer to you, roll the meats and cheeses up like a cigar. Roll tightly, tucking in the peppers and parsley. The "cigar" should be roughly 6 to 8 inches long. Secure the roll by piercing through with toothpicks at every ¾ inch.

Repeat the process for the remaining rollatini.

With a serrated knife, trim ends (for an even look) and cut through the rolls halfway between toothpicks. Keep the toothpicks in place to maintain the pinwheel shapes. Garnish with the remaining teaspoon parsley and a confetti of diced red pepper.

Arrange the rollatini on a platter as hors d'oeuvres, or serve at the table as an appetizer.

Sautéed Calamari with Sun-Dried Tomatoes

SPADELLATA DI CALAMARI

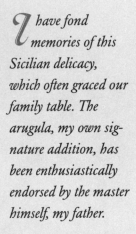

I have fond memories of this Sicilian delicacy, which often graced our family table. The arugula, my own signature addition, has been enthusiastically endorsed by the master himself, my father.

SERVES 6 GENEROUSLY AS APPETIZER

1 pound whole fresh squid (calamari), or ¾ pound cleaned rings
½ cup Italian-Style Bread Crumbs (see page 230)
6 tablespoons olive oil
½ cup chopped onion
6 sun-dried tomatoes packed in oil, thinly sliced
¼ cup pine nuts
2 tablespoons chopped fresh basil
4 cloves garlic, thickly sliced
2 teaspoons grated lemon zest
¼ teaspoon red pepper flakes
¼ teaspoon salt
¼ teaspoon freshly ground black pepper
2 cups chopped arugula (2 bunches)
3 tablespoons freshly squeezed lemon juice

If using whole squid: Rinse thoroughly. Pull the tentacles from the body sac and cut just below the eyes; retain only the leg portion. Turn back the tentacles and squeeze gently to reveal the beadlike beak. Pinch off and discard. Gently squeeze out the viscera from the tubes, and re-move the hard, transparent "quill" that runs the length of the interior wall. Peel the purplish skin from the outside of the tubes. Rinse and pat dry. Slice the tubes into rings and cut the tentacles in half if they are large. Refrigerate until ready to use.

Toss the rings with the bread crumbs. In a large nonstick sauté pan, heat 3 tablespoons olive oil over medium-high heat until the oil sizzles. Pat excess bread crumbs from the squid rings and fry until firm and golden brown, 1 to 2 minutes. Remove from the pan and wipe out any excess crumbs so they do not burn. Heat the remaining 3 tablespoons olive oil over medium-high heat, and add the onion, sun-dried tomatoes, pine nuts, basil, garlic, lemon zest, red pepper flakes, salt, and pepper. Cook until the onion is tender and the pine nuts start to brown, 6 to 8 minutes. Return the squid rings to the pan and toss until well coated with the onion mixture and just cooked through, about 2 minutes more.

Toss with the arugula and lemon juice until the arugula wilts slightly. Serve.

Scallops on a Bed of Leeks and Artichokes

CAPESANTE CON CARCIOFI E PORRI

SERVES 6

10 tablespoons olive oil

6 cloves garlic, thickly sliced

¼ teaspoon red pepper flakes

6 fresh artichoke hearts, thinly sliced (see tip page 16)

6 leeks, white bulb only, thinly sliced, rinsed and drained well

4 tablespoons chopped fresh parsley

¾ teaspoon salt, plus to taste

¾ teaspoon pepper

½ cup brandy

2½ cups Chicken Stock (see page 231)

½ cup heavy cream

4 tablespoons unsalted butter, cut in ½-inch pieces

6 large sea scallops, tough connector muscle removed, sliced in half horizontally if large

Truffle oil (optional)

The first time I wanted to impress my mother by showing her what a good chef I had become, I made this dish for her. She took a bite, smiled at me, and said, "Bravo, Nicolino!" Needless to say, I am quite proud of it.

In a large nonstick pan, heat 8 tablespoons of the olive oil over medium heat. Add the garlic and red pepper flakes and cook until the garlic starts to brown, about 3 to 4 minutes. Add the artichoke hearts, leeks, and parsley, and cook, stirring well, for 5 minutes. Add the salt and pepper, and stir well for 1 minute.

Carefully pour in the brandy to deglaze the pan; stand back, as the brandy will flame up. Once the flames subside, after about a minute, stir well to dislodge any browned bits at the bottom of the pan and cook for 2 to 3 minutes, until the liquid is reduced by half. Add the Chicken Stock and cream, bring to a boil, reduce to a simmer, and cook for 12 minutes.

Five minutes before the mixture is finished cooking, prepare the scallops in a separate nonstick pan: Heat the remaining 2 tablespoons olive oil over high heat until almost smoking. Add the scallops and cook for 1 minute per side. Remove to a bowl and cover with foil to keep warm. Pour off the oil from the pan.

Strain the artichoke-leek mixture; save the liquid sauce. Place an equal portion of the mixture in the middle of each of 6 dishes.

Pour the sauce into the pan in which you cooked the scallops, and bring to a boil, stirring well. Add the scallops and cook for 3 minutes.

Place a scallop on top of the artichoke-leek mixture in each of the dishes. Cook the sauce over high heat for 2 to 3 minutes. Turn off heat and add the butter a piece at a time, stirring well to incorporate into the sauce. Taste for salt, and add if needed. Spoon the sauce into the dishes and top with a few drops of truffle oil if desired.

Scallops with Prosciutto and Morels

CAPESANTE CON PROSCIUTTO E FUNGHI DI BOSCO

SERVES 6 GENEROUSLY

This elegant dish reaches impressive culinary heights while maintaining simple roots. The portions are slightly larger than for usual appetizers—this might even be a small entree.

1 ½ cups Chicken Stock (see page 231)

½ cup dried morel mushrooms (see tip below)

1 recipe Pea Sauce (see page 246)

2 pounds large sea scallops, tough connector muscle removed, sliced in half horizontally if very large

½ teaspoon salt

¾ teaspoon freshly ground black pepper

3 tablespoons olive oil

3 ounces prosciutto or ham, thinly sliced and then chopped

½ cup finely chopped onion

4 cloves garlic, chopped

4 tablespoons brandy

1 to 2 tablespoons butter (optional)

1 tablespoon chopped fresh Italian parsley

Heat the stock and pour over the mushrooms. Let soak for at least 30 minutes to reconstitute. Drain the mushrooms; reserve the stock. Cut the morels in quarters.

Make the Pea Sauce, and while it is cooking, pat the scallops dry and toss with ¼ teaspoon of the salt and ¼ teaspoon of the pepper. In a large sauté pan, heat 2 tablespoons of the olive oil over medium-high heat until sizzling. Sear half of the scallops until golden brown, about 1 minute per side. Remove the scallops with a slotted spoon and repeat for the rest.

In the same pan, with heat reduced to medium, sauté the morels, prosciutto, and onion in the remaining olive oil. Cook until the onion softens and starts to brown, 5 to 6 minutes. Stir in the garlic and cook another minute. Carefully add the brandy to deglaze the pan; stir gently to dislodge any browned bits at the bottom of the pan, and cook to reduce the liquid by half. Add the reserved stock and the remaining ½ teaspoon each salt and pepper. Bring to a boil, then simmer to reduce by half, 4 to 5 minutes. Return the scallops and any accumulated juices to the pan and reheat in the mushroom mixture until just warmed through. Melt in the butter, if desired, for a flavorful glisten.

To serve, spoon the Pea Sauce onto a serving dish and spoon the scallop mixture into the center. Sprinkle with parsley. Serve hot.

Chef's Tip

Use dried chanterelles or porcini for an interesting flavor variation.

Fried Shrimp with Pine Nuts and Herbs

GAMBERI FRITTI CON PINOLI E ERBE

SERVES 6

1¼ cups pine nuts, finely chopped or ground in a food processor (be careful
   not to overprocess)
¼ cup plus 1 tablespoon finely chopped fresh parsley
2 tablespoons finely chopped fresh basil
¾ cup flour
4 teaspoons finely chopped or grated lemon zest
1½ pounds medium shrimp, peeled and deveined, tails left on
4 tablespoons flour for dusting
Egg wash (2 eggs whisked well with 2 teaspoons water)
½ cup extra-light olive oil
Salt and pepper to taste
1 recipe Roasted Garlic and Sun-Dried Tomato Mayonnaise (see page 256)

Here is a Sicilian take on fried shrimp that will make your dinner guests' mouths water.

In a bowl, mix the pine nuts, ¼ cup of the parsley, basil, flour, and lemon zest.

Place in a line in front of you the shrimp, flour, egg wash, pine nut mixture, and two plates, one for coating the shrimp and one, lined with a paper towel, to hold the cooked shrimp. You will have to coat and cook the shrimp in batches, so an assembly line works well.

In a deep, wide sauté pan with a thick bottom, heat the olive oil over medium-high heat. Season the shrimp with salt and pepper to taste—a light sprinkling of each. Dust lightly with flour, and brush off excess. Dip the shrimp in the egg wash, then coat with the pine nut mixture

and place in the hot oil; place only as many as fit comfortably in the pan at one time. Cook for 1 to 1½ minutes per side, until the pine nuts are a light golden, and remove to the plate lined with a paper towel. Continue with the remaining shrimp in as many batches as necessary.

Place the mayonnaise in a small bowl in the center of a platter. Surround with the cooked shrimp. Sprinkle the shrimp with the remaining 1 tablespoon parsley. You might garnish the mayonnaise with a sprig of basil, lemon zest or curls, or a sprig of parsley.

Trio of Stuffed Eggs

Uova sode imbottite

SERVES 6 GENEROUSLY

TUNA-AND-CAPER-STUFFED EGGS

3 hard-boiled eggs, peeled and halved (see tip below)

1 3-ounce can tuna packed in water, drained

3 tablespoons mayonnaise

2 teaspoons plus 1 teaspoon drained capers

1 teaspoon chopped fresh Italian parsley

¼ teaspoon freshly ground black pepper

½ teaspoon anchovy paste (optional)

Spoon the yolks out of the eggs and place in a blender or food processor with the tuna, mayonnaise, 2 teaspoons of the capers, parsley, and pepper, and anchovy paste if desired. Process to a smooth consistency, scraping down the sides of the blender or bowl often. With a spoon or pastry bag, fill the cavities of the egg whites with the tuna mixture. Garnish with the remaining 1 teaspoon capers.

OLIVE-AND-MASCARPONE-STUFFED EGGS

3 hard-boiled eggs, peeled and halved

3 tablespoons mascarpone cheese

3 tablespoons mayonnaise

1 teaspoon chopped fresh Italian parsley

¼ teaspoon freshly ground black pepper

⅛ teaspoon salt

6 to 8 green or Kalamata olives, pitted and chopped, plus 6 slices

Spoon the yolks out of the eggs and place in a blender or food processor with the mascarpone, mayonnaise, parsley, pepper, and salt. Process to a smooth consistency, scraping down the sides of the blender or bowl often. Stir in the chopped olives. With a spoon or pastry bag, fill the cavities of the egg whites with the olive mixture. Garnish with the olive slices.

TRUFFLED MUSHROOM-STUFFED EGGS

1 tablespoon olive oil
½ cup sliced white button, cremini, or shiitake mushrooms
1 tablespoon chopped fresh Italian parsley
1 clove garlic, minced
Pinch red pepper flakes
3 hard-boiled eggs, peeled and halved
3 tablespoons mascarpone cheese
3 tablespoons mayonnaise
¼ teaspoon truffle oil
¼ teaspoon salt
¼ teaspoon freshly ground black pepper

In a small sauté pan, heat the olive oil over high heat. Add the mushrooms, parsley, garlic, and red pepper flakes and sauté until the mushrooms are golden brown, 4 to 6 minutes. Pick out 6 small, pretty mushroom slices for garnish. Set these and the mixture aside to cool.

Spoon the yolks out of the eggs and place in a blender or food processor with the cooled mushroom mixture, mascarpone, mayonnaise, truffle oil, salt, and pepper. Process to a smooth consistency, scraping down the sides of the blender or bowl often. With a spoon or pastry bag, fill the cavities of the egg whites with the mushroom-mascarpone mixture. Garnish each egg with a mushroom slice.

Chef's Tip

To make perfect hard-boiled eggs for this recipe, place 9 eggs in a large saucepan and cover with about an inch of water. Bring the water to a boil over high heat, then turn down to simmer and cook for 10 minutes. When the eggs are cooked, immediately rinse with cold water to stop the cooking. (For a better shape, pierce the larger end of the egg with a thumbtack before boiling.)

Mushroom and Crêpe Torte

TORTINO DI CRESPELLE E FUNGHI

SERVES 6 TO 8

*2 pounds assorted mushrooms (white button, cremini, shiitake, chanterelles),
    trimmed and thickly sliced*

6 ounces prosciutto or ham, chopped

4 to 6 pieces dry porcini mushrooms, processed to a powder (2 tablespoons)

4 cloves garlic, chopped

2 tablespoons chopped fresh Italian parsley

¼ teaspoon red pepper flakes

4 tablespoons olive oil

½ cup white wine

½ teaspoon salt

½ teaspoon freshly ground black pepper

1 recipe Savory Crêpes (see page 272)

1 recipe Parmesan Béchamel Sauce (see page 243)

½ cup freshly grated Parmesan cheese

1 recipe Parmesan Cheese Sauce (see page 245)

1 cup diced fresh tomatoes

Light crêpes are combined with béchamel and sautéed mushrooms to make a layered torte that, as my aunt Buliti used to say, even a saint would find hard to resist.

Preheat oven to 400°.

Make the crêpes and Parmesan Béchamel Sauce.

In a bowl, mix together the mushrooms, ham, porcini powder, garlic, parsley, and red pepper flakes. Let sit for at least 30 minutes.

In a large sauté pan, heat the olive oil over medium-high heat. Add batches of the mushroom mixture and sear for about 4 to 6 minutes per batch; the mushrooms should be brown and quite dry. Remove each cooked batch into a bowl.

Add the wine to deglaze the pan, and scrape lightly to dislodge any browned bits at the bottom. Continue cooking to reduce the liquid by half. Return the mushroom mixture to the pan and season with the salt and pepper.

Grease the bottom and sides of an 8-inch springform pan. Place 2 cooked crêpes on the bottom and spread with a thin layer, about 2 tablespoons, of Parmesan Béchamel Sauce. Spoon a layer of the mushroom mixture, about ½ cup, on the sauce and sprinkle with about an eighth of the grated Parmesan. Cover with 2 more crêpes and repeat the layering and sprinkling until you reach the top of the pan. Finish the torte by spreading the remaining béchamel sauce on top of the last crêpe and sprinkling with the remaining Parmesan. Bake until the crêpes are warmed through and the top is golden brown, about 25 minutes. While the torte is baking, prepare the Parmesan Cheese sauce.

Let the torte rest for 15 minutes before serving. Cut into 6 or 8 wedges, and serve each topped with the Parmesan Cheese Sauce and diced tomatoes.

Stuffed Calamari

CALAMARI RIPIENI

SERVES 6 GENEROUSLY

3 pounds whole fresh squid (calamari), or 2 pounds cleaned tubes
    and tentacles
4 tablespoons olive oil
1½ cups finely chopped onion
1 cup chopped pine nuts
1 cup raisins, plumped in hot water for 20 minutes, drained and chopped
4 cloves garlic, finely chopped
3 tablespoons chopped fresh Italian parsley
¼ teaspoon salt
¼ teaspoon freshly ground black pepper
1 cup Italian-Style Bread Crumbs (see page 230)
1 egg, lightly beaten
½ cup clam juice
Toothpicks
1 recipe Sea Breeze Tomato Sauce (see page 239)

Preheat oven to 300°.

If using whole squid: Rinse thoroughly. Pull the tentacles from the body sac. (To obtain the ink, remove the slender silver ink sac from the strands connected to the tentacles. Place the ink sacs in a small bowl covered with a few drops of water until ready to use. See also tip below.) Clean the tentacles by cutting just below the eyes; retain only the leg portion. Turn back the tentacles and squeeze gently to reveal the beadlike beak. Pinch off and discard. Gently squeeze out the viscera from the tubes, and remove the hard, transparent "quill" that runs the

This is a typical southern Italian dish. Countless variations are to be found, in every village and town between Naples and Palermo, but this is the version my father taught me before I came to America.

length of the interior wall. Peel the purplish skin from the outside of the tubes. Rinse and pat dry. Refrigerate until ready to use.

In a large sauté pan, heat the olive oil over medium-high heat. Add the onion, pine nuts, raisins, and garlic, and sauté until the onions are soft and cooked through, 8 to 10 minutes. Stir in 2 tablespoons of the parsley, salt, and pepper.

In a medium bowl, combine the onion mixture with the bread crumbs, egg, and clam juice. Chop the squid tentacles and stir into the onion mixture; this is the filling. Stuff the squid tubes with about 2 tablespoons of the filling. You might use a large pastry bag to do this easily; do not overstuff, or the tubes will burst during cooking. Close the tube ends with toothpicks. Refrigerate until ready to cook. Make the Sea Breeze Tomato Sauce.

Pour the sauce into an 11x13-inch baking dish, and arrange the stuffed squid on top. Cover and braise in the oven for 45 minutes, or until the squid is cooked through and tender. Remove the toothpicks. Sprinkle with the remaining 1 tablespoon parsley and serve hot.

Chef's Tip

To make this dish in the more traditional style, stir 5 to 6 drops of squid ink into the tomato sauce before baking. If you're not using whole squid and getting the ink there, you can find it at your local fish market or gourmet shop. Use it carefully: a single teaspoon will blacken an entire gallon of sauce!

Truffled Breadsticks

TOSTINI TRIFOLATI

SERVES 4 TO 6 AS AN APPETIZER

¼ cup olive oil

½ teaspoon truffle oil

1 large loaf crusty Italian bread (preferably a day old), cut lengthwise into
    1-inch slices

½ cup freshly grated Parmesan cheese

½ teaspoon salt

¼ teaspoon freshly ground black pepper

Preheat oven to 400°.

In a small bowl, combine the olive oil and truffle oil. Brush the bread slices lightly with the oil mixture and place on a baking sheet. Sprinkle with Parmesan cheese, salt, and pepper, and toast until golden brown, about 6 minutes. Turn bread slices over and toast the other side. Remove from oven and slice lengthwise into "breadsticks" or cut into crouton-size pieces.

Chef's Tip

For a more flavorful finish, first cut the bread, in either sticks or croutons, mix with the other ingredients, then bake, turning pieces of bread to toast evenly. This requires a bit more work but is well worth it.

A very versatile recipe: these flavorful breadsticks are great as party snacks, give a nice touch at mealtimes, and as croutons are a tasty addition to soups and salads. It all depends on how you cut the bread.

Zio Giovanni

Every once in a while, my wife, Nanci, and I spend an hour or so looking at old family photographs and sharing reminiscences. Recently on one of these occasions, I found a picture of my mother's brother, my uncle Giovanni, holding me up in the air.

In his younger days, Zio had been a great wit and quite dashing—or so his mother, Nonna Adele, and his brother, my uncle Alfredo, were quick to declare. Truth to tell, this is not how I remember him. It seemed that fortunes changed for him after a near-fatal motorcycle accident, which left him slower, yet never short of a great spirit and unbridled enthusiasm for life and family. My uncle could always make us feel happy, dancing us around, singing robustly from his favorite operas and folk songs. With him around, laughter was never far from Nonna's farmhouse. Zio Giovanni never married, and after my grandfather died and all his siblings had moved on, he returned home to help my grandmother.

In 1991, when Zio Giovanni became gravely ill, Nanci and I went to Italy to see him. During one of our visits with him in the hospital, he motioned to me to come sit down next to his bed. As I held his hand he pulled me closer and whispered, "Nicolino, you should not die without following your dreams." He caressed my head and blew me a kiss.

That night the family got together for dinner at Nonna Adele's. The mood was somber, and no one seemed able to smile. As we ate, the only sound to break the silence was that of the silverware against the dishes. For a family so used to raucous mealtimes, the silence was disconcerting.

Then, like a roll of thunder in the distance, my mother started to giggle. As the rest of us paused in mid-forkfuls, her giggles grew into hearty, infectious laughter. Soon we were all laughing so hard we were close to tears. Even though nobody except my mother knew what we were laughing about, it was as if a great dam had burst; no one was able to stop the pent-up emotion from coming out. At that moment, I suppose, it could have been laughter or tears.

Through her laughter my mother managed to stammer, "Do you remember when Giovanni was sixteen . . . that night in the cemetery?"

What happened at the cemetery?" I laughed even harder, although I didn't know why.

Your uncle made a bet with his friends. Oh, God . . . he was wild!" my aunt Titi screamed.

No, no. Let me tell it," my mother begged. And wiping the tears from her face, she began. "Your uncle needed some money to buy a new suit for the Saturday dance, so he bet that band of rascals he called his friends that he could meet any dare they would throw his way. Of course, everybody took him up on it, and put their money into your uncle Alfredo's hat. Then the boys came up with the dare: Giovanni would have to run naked through the cemetery at midnight. There had been rumors of ghosts and other unspeakable things haunting that old graveyard, so everyone was sure your uncle would try to get out of the dare. But Giovanni wasn't one to back down from a challenge, and besides, he must have figured a new suit was worth a few embarrassing moments.

Well, it had been overcast and rainy all day, and later the wind came up. You can imagine, it was a perfect night for a prank like this! By the time the boys made their way to the graveyard around midnight, it was pretty eerie. Giovanni undressed quickly and without a moment's hesitation climbed over the tall gates and started running between the headstones. He was acting like such a clown, running along, flailing his arms—showing off, I guess—that in the darkness he didn't see a big mud hole in the pathway. One minute, there he was, dashing through the cemetery, a white streak against the black night, and the next, he'd vanished. Nobody and nothing moved. Everything was silent except for the trees creaking in the wind.

But your uncle certainly wasn't going to miss an opportunity to get his own back. It took him a couple of minutes to catch his breath, and then he leaped out of the hole and started running back toward the gates, dripping with mud and howling like some kind of wild man. God, he must have looked a fright."

By now my father was laughing so hard that his eyes were closed shut. Aunt Buliti was holding her sides and rocking back and forth in her chair. Nanci, who was only beginning to learn Italian, was laughing harder than anyone, while she held my mother's hand.

Well, those kids really got scared!" my mother continued. "They started to holler and ran off in every direction, taking Zio's clothes with them. So there he was, alone at the gates, with the foul-smelling mud drying on his body like a second skin.

His friends were gone, and there was nobody else around, so he grabbed a few branches from a tree and covered himself the best he could, and ran home. He made it back without meeting anyone, but your grandfather caught him trying to get in through an open window. He wasn't allowed to leave the house for a week. He never made it to the Saturday dance. And to make matters worse, he never got his money. But he couldn't bring himself to go after his friends."

The whole evening went on like this. Everyone told a favorite story. What had started somberly turned into a celebration for a very special man who will forever live in our memories.

Uncle Giovanni died a few weeks later. And shortly afterward, with his last words clear in my head, I quit my job as a stockbroker to follow my own dreams of working in a restaurant. Even though I was starting in the kitchen washing dishes, I know that my uncle would have been proud.

Soups, Salads, and Side Dishes

Cabbage Soup

   Corn, Zucchini, and Pepper Soup

      Fragrant Chicken Soup with Meatballs

         Minestrone

           Mussel Soup with Curry

              Potato Soup with Mortadella and Salami

Green Salad with Broiled Goat Cheese

   Lobster Salad

      Raw Mushroom Salad

         Shrimp and Cannellini Salad

           Rice Salad

              Sautéed Lima Beans

                 Roasted Smashed Potatoes with Peppers

Stewed Peas with Sun-Dried Tomatoes

   Sautéed Mushrooms, Green Beans, Tomatoes,

      and Prosciutto

      Mashed Potatoes Parmesan

         Grandma's Polenta

           Sautéed Spinach

              Saffroned Rice Timbales

Cabbage Soup

ZUPPA DI CAVOLO

SERVES 6 TO 8

3 tablespoons olive oil
1½ cups chopped onion
6 cloves garlic, thickly sliced
¼ teaspoon red pepper flakes
1 medium head green cabbage (Savoy), thinly sliced
1½ teaspoons salt
1 teaspoon freshly ground black pepper
10 cups Beef Stock (see page 233)
1 recipe Truffled Breadsticks (see page 41)
3 tablespoons extra-virgin olive oil
½ cup freshly grated Parmesan cheese

In a soup pot, heat the 3 tablespoons olive oil over medium heat. Add the onion, garlic, and red pepper flakes. Sauté until the onion is light brown and tender, about 6 minutes. Add the cabbage, season with the salt and pepper, and cook until cabbage is just wilted, 2 to 3 minutes. Pour in the stock and bring to a boil, then simmer 5 to 10 minutes to blend the flavors.

To serve, place plenty of Truffled Bread croutons in each of 6 to 8 soup bowls and pour the hot soup on top. Drizzle with the extra-virgin olive oil and sprinkle with the grated cheese.

Here is a Sicilian recipe from the heart of the island. It reminds me of when my family got together at my uncle Mimì and aunt Ciccina's, in the countryside outside Alcamo. You might be tempted to start a tradition in your own family by making this for your next meal.

Corn, Zucchini, and Pepper Soup

ZUPPA DI MAIS, ZUCCHINE E PEPERONI

SERVES 6

This soup has been made by at least three generations of my family. I hope that you'll be making it too.

3 tablespoons olive oil

6 large cloves garlic

½ teaspoon red pepper flakes

6 ounces pancetta or bacon, (2 thick slices about ⅜ inch thick), cut into
    ¼-inch dice

2 medium leeks, white bulb only, sliced into thin rounds, rinsed and
    drained well

2 small or 1 large zucchini (about ¾ pound), cut in half and thinly sliced or
    cut into eighths lengthwise and then into small chunks

1 large red bell pepper, core, seeds, and membranes removed, sliced into thin
    bite-size strips

1 15-ounce can whole corn, rinsed and well drained

½ teaspoon dried thyme

6 cups Chicken Stock (see page 231)

⅔ cup heavy cream

½ cup chopped fresh parsley, plus 2 tablespoons for garnish

Tabasco sauce (optional; see tip below)

⅔ cup freshly grated Parmesan cheese

1 recipe Truffled Breadsticks, cut as croutons (optional; see page 41)

In a Dutch oven, heat 2 tablespoons of the olive oil over medium-high heat. Add the garlic, red pepper flakes, pancetta, and leeks. Sauté until the garlic and pancetta are light brown, about 5 minutes. Add the zucchini, bell pepper, corn, and thyme. Sauté for 5 minutes. Add the stock and cream. Bring to a boil, then reduce heat and simmer, uncovered, for 15 to 20 minutes.

Stir in the ½ cup parsley, Tabasco if desired, and half the cheese. Place plenty of Truffled Bread croutons in each of 6 soup bowls, if desired, and pour the hot soup on top. Sprinkle with the 2 tablespoons parsley and the remaining cheese.

Chef's Tip

If you do use Tabasco sauce, you may want to decrease the red pepper flakes to ¼ teaspoon.

Fragrant Chicken Soup with Meatballs

POLPETTINE DI POLLO IN UMIDO

SERVES 6 TO 8

CHICKEN MEATBALLS

1 pound ground chicken (preferably dark meat)

4 cloves garlic, chopped

1 ¼ cups Italian-Style Bread Crumbs (see page 230)

½ cup freshly grated Romano cheese

2 tablespoons milk

1 medium egg

1 tablespoon chopped fresh parsley

CHICKEN SOUP

6 tablespoons olive oil

1 cup peeled, finely diced carrot

½ cup chopped onion

6 cloves garlic, thickly sliced

¼ teaspoon red pepper flakes

¼ teaspoon dry thyme

¼ teaspoon dry sage

⅛ teaspoon dry marjoram

⅛ teaspoon dry oregano

¼ teaspoon salt

¼ teaspoon freshly ground black pepper

½ cup barley

2 tablespoons chopped fresh parsley

12 cups Chicken Stock (see page 231)

½ cup freshly grated Parmesan cheese (optional)

With its full-bodied, flavorful broth, this is delightfully comforting on a cool autumn evening.

In a large bowl, combine the ingredients for the meatballs. Mix with your hands, stirring well to incorporate, until you have a large, uniform meatball. From this make 21 small meatballs, about 2 inches long and 1½ inches wide. Place them in a bowl, cover, and set aside.

In a large saucepan heat the olive oil over medium heat. Add the carrot, onion, garlic, red pepper flakes, dry herbs, salt, and pepper. Cook for 10 minutes, stirring well every 5 minutes. Add the barley and parsley, stir well, and cook 5 minutes. Add the stock, increase heat to high, then simmer for 15 minutes, stirring well every 5 minutes.

Bring the stock back to a boil over high heat, add the meatballs one at a time, stirring well to prevent them from sticking to the bottom of the pan. Cook for 5 minutes. Reduce to a simmer and cook, almost covered, for 20 minutes, stirring well every 10 minutes. Uncover and simmer for 40 minutes, stirring well every 10 minutes.

Serve in deep bowls, and top each with 1 tablespoon grated Parmesan cheese if desired.

Chef's Tip

The importance of stirring

Stirring "well" might appear to be nothing more than a tedious chore. However repetitive it may seem, it *is* important if you want your ingredients to cook evenly. By stirring properly you prevent food from sticking to the bottom of the pan, especially when cooking over high heat. To me, stirring fulfills a need to be connected with the food I am preparing. Sometimes, I imagine that I am a maestro conducting a symphony of culinary delights. To add drama to the process, often I bang on the side of the pan while I stir, as if keeping tempo. While this may do absolutely nothing to improve the flavor, it does impress casual onlookers.

Minestrone

SERVES 6

I won't lie to you: when I was a child I was not crazy about minestrone. Like many children, I did just about everything in my power to avoid vegetables. It was not until my later teens that I discovered the magic of this soup. My mother attributes all sorts of restorative powers to it, but then all mothers in Italy say that about their own minestrone. I must admit that whenever I feel sick, a bowl of minestrone works magic on me.

3 tablespoons olive oil

4 ounces pancetta or bacon, cut into ¼-inch dice

¼ teaspoon red pepper flakes

4 medium cloves garlic, thickly sliced

1 cup diced white onion, cut into ½-inch dice

1 cup diced celery, cut into ¼-inch dice

1 cup diced carrot, cut into ¼-inch dice

1 teaspoon very finely chopped fresh rosemary

1 teaspoon thinly sliced fresh sage

2 tablespoons chopped fresh parsley

2 tablespoons thinly sliced fresh basil

2 medium potatoes, peeled and cut into ½-inch dice

2 cups diced zucchini, cut into ¼-inch dice

8 cups chicken stock, homemade (see page 231) or canned

1½ cups Tomato Sauce (see page 235)

½ teaspoon freshly ground black pepper

Salt to taste

½ cup Arborio rice

1 cup rinsed and drained canned cannellini beans

6 teaspoons freshly grated Parmesan cheese

6 tablespoons extra-virgin olive oil (optional)

In a large stockpot, heat 2 tablespoons of the olive oil over medium heat. Add the pancetta, red pepper flakes, and garlic. Cook for 3 to 4 minutes. Add the remaining tablespoon of olive oil, onion, celery, carrot, and herbs. Sauté, stirring well, until the onion is soft and translucent, about 5 to 7 minutes. Add the potatoes and zucchini. Toss well with other vegetables to coat with the oil and herbs. Sauté for 2 to 3 minutes. Add the stock, Tomato Sauce, and pepper. Stir well.

Bring to a boil, reduce heat, cover, and simmer for 20 to 25 minutes, or until the vegetables are tender. Taste for salt. If the pancetta is salty and you used canned stock, you won't need to add salt.

Add the rice, stir, cover, and simmer for 15 to 20 minutes. Add the cannellini, cover, and simmer for 5 minutes.

Ladle the soup generously into 6 bowls. Sprinkle each with 1 teaspoon Parmesan cheese, and drizzle a tablespoon of the extra-virgin olive oil over each if desired.

Mussel Soup with Curry

ZUPPA DI COZZE AL CURRY

SERVES 6 GENEROUSLY

2½ pounds fresh mussels
4 tablespoons olive oil
½ cup finely chopped onion
4 cloves garlic, thickly sliced
1 tablespoon curry powder
1 tablespoon finely chopped lemon zest
¼ teaspoon red pepper flakes (optional)
1 cup sparkling white wine
3 cups clam juice
1 cup heavy cream
2 cups peeled, diced white potato, cut into ½-inch dice
¼ teaspoon salt
¼ teaspoon freshly ground black pepper
2 tablespoons thinly sliced fresh basil

My father built quite a reputation with this dish. I borrowed the recipe and have had it with me in every restaurant where I worked. The inclusion of curry in an Italian dish may seem unusual, but for the Venetians, who were great traders with the Far East, it is not uncommon.

Pull the mossy "beard" from each mussel and scrub the shell well. Discard any mussels that do not close tightly when tapped. Chill the mussels until ready to use.

In a soup pot, heat the olive oil over medium-low heat. Add the onion and garlic and sauté over medium heat, slowly, until the onion is golden and soft, about 8 to 10 minutes. Stir in the curry powder and lemon zest, and the red pepper flakes if desired, and cook 1 minute.

Add the mussels to the pot and increase heat to high. Toss well. Pour in the wine and simmer, covered, for 3 to 4 minutes. Uncover and remove the mussels to a large bowl as they open. Discard any that have not opened after 6 to 7 minutes. When the mussels have been removed, add the clam juice, cream, potato, salt, and pepper. Cover and simmer for 20 minutes, or until the potatoes are tender.

While the soup is cooking, remove the mussels from their shells. Pour any liquid that has accumulated in the mussel bowl into the soup.

When the soup has finished cooking, puree it to a smooth cream in a food processor or blender. Reheat the soup on low heat. Stir in the mussels and the basil. Serve immediately.

Chef's Tip

A medium-hot curry mix will give a nice spicy balance to this dish. If you don't like curry, use turmeric instead, to obtain the yellowish color. The optional ¼ teaspoon red pepper flakes makes the dish spicier.

Potato Soup with Mortadella and Salami

ZUPPA DEI MONACI

SERVES 6 TO 8

Legend has it that mortadella (something like bologna) was invented in a Franciscan monastery in Emilia-Romagna. Hence the Italian name of this dish, which translates as "monks' soup." It tastes great and will nourish both body and soul. Add a light salad and a glass of Chianti and you'll have a whole meal!

4 tablespoons olive oil

8 ounces salami, chopped

8 ounces mortadella or bologna, chopped

1 cup chopped onion

4 cloves garlic, thickly sliced

2 tablespoons chopped fresh Italian parsley

½ teaspoon red pepper flakes

1 14.5-ounce can Italian-style stewed tomatoes, drained and chopped, juice reserved

4 cups peeled, diced white potato, cut into ½-inch dice (about 2 pounds)

6 cups Chicken Stock (see page 231)

¼ teaspoon salt

½ teaspoon freshly ground black pepper

½ cup heavy cream

1 cup freshly grated Parmesan cheese

6 to 8 fresh basil leaves, thinly sliced

6 teaspoons extra-virgin olive oil

In a large soup pot, heat the 4 tablespoons olive oil over medium heat. Add the salami, mortadella, onion, garlic, parsley, and red pepper flakes and cook until the onion is tender, 8 to 10 minutes. Add the tomatoes and cook 3 to 4 minutes, stirring often. Add the potatoes, stock, reserved tomato juice, salt, and pepper. Bring to a boil, reduce heat, cover, and simmer until the potatoes are tender, about 30 minutes. Add the cream, stir well, and cook 5 minutes.

Remove from heat and stir in ¾ cup of the cheese.

Serve in large bowls topped with the remaining cheese, sliced basil, and a drizzle of extra-virgin olive oil.

Chef's Tip

I love this hearty meat-and-potato soup pureed to a thick cream and served with cheese and olive oil. Toast some thickly sliced day-old bread, and rub on both sides with a peeled garlic clove. Place the toast at the bottom of the soup bowl and pour the pureed soup on top.

Green Salad with Broiled Goat Cheese

INSALATA CON FORMAGGIO CAPRINO

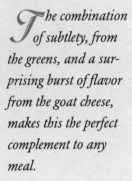

SERVES 6

The combination of subtlety, from the greens, and a surprising burst of flavor from the goat cheese, makes this the perfect complement to any meal.

12 ounces mixed salad greens
1 teaspoon salt
1 teaspoon freshly ground black pepper
4 tablespoons extra-virgin olive oil
2 ½ tablespoons balsamic vinegar
6 slices baguette bread, cut 1 inch thick
1 1-pound log fresh goat cheese

Preheat oven broiler.

Place the salad greens in a large bowl, sprinkle with the salt and pepper, and mix well. Add 2 tablespoons of the olive oil and 1 tablespoon of the vinegar, and toss the salad until well coated.

Toast the bread in a toaster oven, and while it is toasting cut the cheese into 6 equal slices no more than 1½ inches thick. Place a piece of cheese on each slice of toast, then bake under the broiler until the cheese starts to brown on top.

Place the pieces of toast and broiled cheese in the middle of the salad, and serve. For a stronger flavor, drizzle salad serving with the remaining olive oil and vinegar.

Chef's Tip

By adding the salt and pepper to the salad before the oil and vinegar, you ensure a better seasoning. When you add the oil and vinegar, mix the salad well, with your hands rather than tools; you'll be surprised at how much better you can mix it. Regulate the oil and vinegar to your own taste.

Lobster Salad

INSALATA RUSSA

SERVES 6

3 cups peeled, diced new potatoes, cut into ½-inch dice (about 4 medium)

2 cups trimmed string beans, sliced diagonally into 1-inch pieces (½ to ¾ pound, before trimming)

1 cup peeled, sliced carrots, sliced into ¼-inch half-moons (about 3 medium)

1 cup fresh or frozen peas, plus additional for garnish if desired

1 cup drained canned diced beets, plus additional for garnish if desired

4 cups fresh or frozen lobster meat (if frozen, thawed and well drained)

2 tablespoons drained small capers

1 cup mayonnaise (your favorite brand or homemade; see page 255)

2 teaspoons freshly squeezed lemon juice

¼ teaspoon salt

Lettuce leaves, washed and well dried

6 lemon wedges

6 empty lobster tails, optional

Bring a pot of water, salted if desired, to a boil. Add potatoes and cook al dente—firm, slightly undercooked—3 to 4 minutes. Bring a second pot of salted water to a boil. Add the string beans and cook al dente, 3 to 4 minutes. Remove with a slotted spoon. Add the carrots to the water and cook al dente, 3 to 4 minutes. Remove with a slotted spoon. Add peas to the water. Boil for 1 minute. Remove with a slotted spoon. Drain all the vegetables, including the potatoes, well and cool.

In a large bowl, combine the cooled cooked vegetables, beets, and lobster meat. In a smaller bowl, combine the capers and mayonnaise, mashing the capers into the mayonnaise with a fork. Add the mayonnaise mixture to the vegetable mixture and toss to coat.

My brother and I were a pair of devilish terrors, but there was nothing we wouldn't do, including turn into our mother's "good little boys," if we knew it would earn us an extra helping of this heavenly dish. The addition of the lobster to a classic Russian salad was an innovation that spoke to my family's love of crustaceans.

Just before serving, refresh with the lemon juice and salt. Toss well.

Line a platter or individual plates with the lettuce leaves. Mound the salad on the lettuce and garnish with the lemon wedges. For a more formal presentation, spoon the salad into 6 empty lobster tails laid over lettuce leaves, and decorate the top of each with peas and beets.

Chef's Tip

My mother used to mix the beets into the salad, and I highly endorse this practice. Be aware, however, that the beets will leak and turn the salad pink. If you mind the odd color, instead of mixing the beets into the salad, sprinkle them around the edge just before serving.

Raw Mushroom Salad

INSALATA DI FUNGHI

SERVES 6 TO 8

This wonderful recipe enhances all the qualities of even the most common mushrooms. As one of my dinner companions once exclaimed, "The marinade makes the mushrooms sing opera!" Note that you'll need ½ pound each of the three types of mushrooms.

MARINADE

½ teaspoon Dijon mustard

4 flat anchovy fillets packed in oil, drained

½ cup freshly squeezed lemon juice

2 teaspoons sherry vinegar

½ teaspoon salt

Freshly ground black pepper to taste

1 cup olive oil

SALAD

½ pound each cremini, white, and shiitake mushrooms, brushed clean, stems
   trimmed, sliced ⅛ inch thick

3 tablespoons chopped fresh parsley

3 tablespoons thinly sliced basil leaves

1 large red bell pepper, finely diced

8 ounces salad greens, washed and well dried

½ large head red-leaf lettuce, cleaned and well dried (about ½ pound)

1 head Boston lettuce, cleaned and well dried (about ¼ pound)

8 ounces Parmesan cheese, shaved (see tip below)

Make the marinade: Put the mustard, anchovies, lemon juice, vinegar, salt, and pepper in a food processor. Process until smooth. With the machine running, drizzle in the olive oil.

Make the salad: In a large bowl, mix the mushrooms, parsley, basil, and bell pepper with 1 cup of the marinade. Toss well to moisten the mushrooms. Allow to marinate for 1 hour, tossing every 30 minutes.

Dress the salad greens with some of the remaining marinade, a few tablespoons at a time, until dressed to your liking. Place the dressed greens on a platter. Top with the marinated mushrooms and shaved Parmesan.

Chef's Tip

To shave Parmesan, you need a solid piece of cheese and an ordinary swivel potato peeler. Scrape the peeler against the cheese as if you were peeling potatoes. You will obtain Parmesan shavings, a fun alternative to grated cheese.

Shrimp and Cannellini Salad

INSALATA DI MARE

SERVES 6 TO 8

The flavors in this salad are light and balanced. With a glass of good Chardonnay it makes a refreshing summer lunch.

6 tablespoons olive oil

5 tablespoons freshly squeezed lemon juice

¼ teaspoon white pepper

½ teaspoon salt

3 tablespoons finely chopped fresh oregano, or 1 tablespoon dried

2 pounds medium shrimp boiled, peeled, and chilled

2 15-ounce cans cannellini (or Great Northern) beans, rinsed and drained

¾ cup chopped fresh fennel (see tip below)

¼ cup chopped fresh Italian parsley

1 cup finely chopped white onion

1 cup diced yellow bell pepper, cut into ¼-inch dice

1 cup diced red bell peppers, cut into ¼-inch dice

1½ cups seeded, chopped Roma (pear) tomatoes, or other firm tomatoes

½ cup pitted, chopped Greek or Sicilian black olives (optional)

1 tablespoon minced fresh garlic

Salt and pepper to taste

8 ounces mixed lettuces, washed and well dried

Whisk the olive oil and lemon juice together. Add the white pepper, salt, and oregano. In a separate bowl, combine the remaining ingredients except for the salt and pepper. Toss with the olive oil dressing, add salt and pepper to taste, and refrigerate for at least 1 hour to allow flavors to blend.

Remove from refrigerator and let sit. Serve the dish chilled rather than ice cold. You might serve over a bed of mixed lettuces.

Chef's Tip

To prepare fresh fennel: Rinse thoroughly, and trim stalks to within ½ inch of the bulb. Peel away the tough outer stalks, and cut the tender interior of the bulb in half lengthwise, then slice crosswise. In this recipe, if fresh fennel is not available, use celery.

Rice Salad

INSALATA DI RISO

SERVES 6

Ideal for your next summer picnic, this salad is fresh and tangy, and goes well with a variety of entrees. I particularly recommend serving it with Veal Tonnato (see page 186).

6 quarts water

1½ teaspoons salt

1½ cups Arborio rice

1 recipe Mustard Vinaigrette (see page 254)

1 large tomato, seeded and diced

12 asparagus spears, steamed or boiled al dente, sliced diagonally into
*   ¾-inch pieces, tips left whole*

¾ cup chopped fresh parsley

1 4-ounce jar marinated white button mushrooms, drained and halved

1 6-ounce jar artichoke hearts, drained and cut into 1-inch pieces

2 hard-boiled eggs, finely chopped

2 tablespoons sherry vinegar or white wine vinegar

2 tablespoons freshly squeezed lemon juice

Bring the water, with 1 teaspoon of the salt, to a rapid boil. Add the rice. Stir once, gently. Bring again to a boil and cook for 10 to 12 minutes; after 8 or 9 minutes, taste a grain or two, and continue tasting until it is al dente (firm but not hard in the center). When cooked al dente, drain well. Transfer to a glass bowl and toss with the Mustard Vinaigrette. Allow to cool.

When rice has cooled, combine in a large bowl with tomato, asparagus, parsley, mushrooms, artichoke hearts, and eggs. Refrigerate for at least 1 hour. Just before serving, combine vinegar, lemon juice, and remaining ½ teaspoon salt. Splash over the salad, toss, and serve.

Chef's Tip

You can spike this salad with just about anything you want. Let me throw a few ideas at you: boiled shrimp, diced ham, barbecued sausage, diced grilled tuna, chopped prosciutto . . .

Sautéed Lima Beans

SPADELLATA DI FAVETTE

SERVES 6

4 tablespoons olive oil
4 cloves garlic, thickly sliced
¼ teaspoon red pepper flakes
4 tablespoons chopped fresh parsley
2 teaspoons finely chopped rosemary
1 cup diced white onion (about ½ large onion)
2 10-ounce packages frozen lima beans
½ teaspoon salt
¼ teaspoon freshly ground black pepper
3 tablespoons freshly squeezed lemon juice
1 cup Chicken Stock (see page 231)

Although this Sicilian recipe is usually made with fava beans, I chose lima because they are more readily available. The dish is simple to prepare and the flavor combinations surprising, so you'll probably be serving this regularly.

In a deep, wide sauté pan, heat the olive oil over medium-high heat. Add the garlic, red pepper flakes, 3 tablespoons of the parsley, rosemary, and onion. Cook until the onion starts to soften, about 5 minutes. Add the beans and cook, stirring well, for about 2 minutes. Season with the salt and pepper.

Add the lemon juice and stock, stirring well. Bring to a boil, then reduce heat and simmer, covered, until beans are done, 9 to 10 minutes. Add salt to taste.

There will be some flavorful liquid in the bottom of the pan; spoon this over the beans. Sprinkle with the remaining 1 tablespoon parsley and serve.

Roasted Smashed Potatoes with Peppers

PASTICCIO DI PATATE ARROSTO CON PEPERONI

SERVES 6 TO 8

3 pounds potatoes (preferably Yukon), unpeeled, cut in 1-inch cubes
1 teaspoon salt
¼ teaspoon freshly ground black pepper
½ teaspoon dried thyme
6 tablespoons olive oil
2 yellow bell peppers, cut in 1-inch pieces
2 red bell peppers, cut in 1-inch pieces
1 medium onion, thinly sliced
2 cups Chicken Stock (see page 231)
½ cup freshly grated Romano cheese
¼ cup freshly grated Parmesan cheese (optional)

Preheat oven to 450°.

In a large bowl, mix the potatoes with ½ teaspoon of the salt, the pepper, thyme, and 4 tablespoons of the olive oil. Grease a large glass baking dish with 1 tablespoon of the olive oil. Spread the seasoned potatoes in the dish, and bake for 30 minutes. After that time, turn the potatoes with a spatula or a long-handled cooking spoon. Some will stick to the bottom and break; don't worry, that's supposed to happen. Bake for 10 more minutes.

Meanwhile, in a large bowl, mix the bell peppers and onion with the remaining ½ teaspoon salt and the remaining tablespoon olive oil. Add

These are not your typical roasted potatoes. The texture is more like that of mashed potatoes, so you don't have to be careful when you're stirring this up: if the potatoes start to break up, they're doing what's intended. Do not use a metal baking sheet for this; a glass baking dish is best.

to the potatoes in the baking dish, and as you do this, the potatoes will break even more. Bake for 35 minutes.

Remove from oven and add the stock, mixing well. As you stir, dislodge any browned bits stuck to the bottom of the dish. Sprinkle the Romano cheese on top and bake for 10 minutes. Again remove from the oven, stir well, and dislodge any browned bits at the bottom of the dish. Let rest for 5 minutes, sprinkle the Parmesan on top if desired, and serve.

Chef's Tip

You can make this recipe with any type of potato you like: Yukon is what I prefer. If you use another type, you may have to adjust the cooking times to accommodate the different size and texture. You cannot overcook this dish, but if you don't stir the ingredients during the cooking as instructed, you may end up with burned potatoes at the bottom of the baking dish. When adding stock, you are effectively deglazing the dish; this will help enormously in softening and dislodging any brown crust that may form.

Different ovens distribute heat with different intensity; a gas oven and an electric oven function differently. Trust your instincts and your senses rather than the numbers on the dial. If you have an electric oven, do not put the baking dish too close to the heating rods at the bottom, or you'll end up with char-roasted potatoes!

And in case you're wondering, I prefer to keep the skin on the potatoes because that's how it was done in my family's kitchen.

Stewed Peas with Sun-Dried Tomatoes

PISELLI STUFATI CON POMODORI SECCHI

SERVES 6 TO 8 AS A SIDE DISH OR AN APPETIZER

5 tablespoons olive oil
8 cloves garlic, thickly sliced
2 cups chopped onion
3 tablespoons chopped sun-dried tomatoes packed in olive oil, drained before chopping
2¼ cups frozen peas
½ teaspoon salt

Pour the oil into a saucepan, add the garlic, and cook over medium heat for 3 to 5 minutes, until the garlic starts to brown. Add the onion and sun-dried tomatoes and cook for 15 minutes, stirring every 5 minutes. Add the peas, and stir well to incorporate the ingredients. Cook for 35 to 40 minutes, almost covered.

Add the salt and stir well. Place in a serving bowl and bring to the table.

With its rich flavor, this dish is sure to please the most discriminating tastes. Even the kids will eat up their vegetables when they're served like this. For an extraspecial indulgence, add toasted pine nuts just before serving. This dish tastes even better when prepared a day in advance, refrigerated, and gently reheated just before serving.

Sautéed Mushrooms, Green Beans, Tomatoes, and Prosciutto

SPADELLATA DI FUNGHI, FAGIOLINI, POMODORI E PROSCIUTTO

SERVES 6 TO 8 AS A SIDE DISH OR AN APPETIZER

This dish is so simple it might become a fixture at your family dinners. The array of colors and flavors will make you shine like a master chef.

1 pound cherry tomatoes, cut in halves
¼ teaspoon salt
¼ teaspoon sugar
1 pound green beans, trimmed at the ends
½ cup olive oil
8 cloves garlic, thickly sliced
1 pound small cremini mushrooms, cut in halves
½ cup white wine
¼ teaspoon red pepper flakes
4 ounces prosciutto or ham, chopped
2 tablespoons chopped fresh parsley

Sprinkle the cut side of the cherry tomatoes with the salt and sugar. Set aside.

Bring a large pot of water to a boil over high heat. Add the green beans and cook for 7 to 8 minutes. Drain and cool with cold water. Set aside.

Pour ¼ cup of the olive oil into a 12-inch nonstick skillet, then add the garlic and cook over medium heat for 3 to 5 minutes, until the garlic starts to brown. Add the mushrooms and cook for 10 minutes, stirring every 5 minutes. Increase heat to high and deglaze the pan with the wine, scraping gently to dislodge any browned bits from the bottom. Cook for 5 minutes. Remove the cooked mushrooms to large bowl, and cover to keep warm.

Wipe the skillet clean, and in it heat the remaining ¼ cup olive oil over high heat until sizzling. Add the cherry tomatoes, reduce heat to medium, and cook for 5 minutes. Add the green beans, red pepper flakes, and prosciutto. Cook for 5 minutes, stirring well. Add the parsley, again stirring well, and cook for 2 minutes. Add this mixture to the mushrooms in the bowl, and stir well to incorporate all the ingredients. Serve hot or at room temperature.

Mashed Potatoes Parmesan

PURÈ DI PATATE ALLA PARMIGIANA

SERVES 6

There are mashed potatoes, and then there are mashed potatoes. For me this is the ultimate comfort food, almost better than chocolate. And for me, that's saying a lot!

1 tablespoon kosher salt
3½ pounds potatoes, peeled and cut into 2-to-3-inch chunks
1 recipe Parmesan Béchamel Sauce, warm (see page 243)
2 tablespoons freshly chopped basil
2 tablespoons butter (optional)
Salt and pepper to taste

Bring a large pot of water to a boil, enough to cover the potatoes by at least 2 inches. Add the salt and potatoes and cook for about 20 minutes. (Check for tenderness after 15 minutes; you want the potatoes soft enough to mash easily but not fall apart.) When cooked, strain and return to pot. Rice or mash the potatoes. Stir in the béchamel and the basil. Taste. If you would like this to be even richer, add the butter and stir well. Salt and pepper to taste.

Chef's Tip

For another presentation of the recipe, spoon the prepared mashed potatoes into a gratin dish. Sprinkle the top with 2 tablespoons freshly grated Parmesan cheese and broil in the oven for 2 to 3 minutes, until the top is golden brown. This adds a nice color and texture–a crunch.

Grandma's Polenta

POLENTA DELLA NONNA

SERVES 6

1 16-ounce box instant polenta
1 cup freshly grated Parmesan cheese
8 ounces mascarpone or cream cheese
½ teaspoon freshly ground black pepper

Prepare the polenta according to the directions on the package. When it is almost cooked through, remove from heat. (The polenta should be fairly loose, so that it accepts the cheeses easily.) Stir in the cheeses and pepper. Serve alongside your favorite main dish.

Chef's Tip

As an alternative, spread the prepared polenta on a well-greased baking sheet, about 1 inch high, and leave it to cool and harden. When it has, cut into squares, triangles, or any other shape you wish. (At this point, the cut polenta can be refrigerated for several days or frozen; thaw and heat before using.) Brush the pieces of polenta with olive oil. They can be barbecued, sautéed, broiled, or roasted—each technique resulting in a different flavor experience.

During the Second World War, my grandma Adele had to make do with whatever was available to feed the family. Sometimes cornmeal was all there was, but she always found interesting ways to prepare this rustic dish. Here is one of my mother's favorites.

Sautéed Spinach

SPADELLATA DI SPINACI

SERVES 6

*B*ada-bing,
bada-boom,
bada-bang, and you're
done! You can't beat
this old-fashioned
country style of prepar-
ing fresh spinach.

4 bunches (about 1 pound) fresh spinach, washed, rinsed, and dried, thick
    stems removed
3 tablespoons olive oil
¼ teaspoon salt
¼ teaspoon freshly ground black pepper
1 tablespoon freshly squeezed lemon juice (optional)

Place the spinach in a large bowl, sprinkle the salt and pepper over it, and mix well with your hands.

In a large sauté pan, heat the olive oil over medium-high heat. Add the spinach and sauté for 2 to 3 minutes, until the spinach collapses. Add the lemon juice if desired, and mix well. Serve.

Chef's Tip

Believe it or not, the best pan for this recipe is a nonstick wok. The sides are high enough so that when you toss the spinach, it won't spill over. In addition, the heat is uniformly distributed and the nonstick surface prevents scorching.

Saffroned Rice Timbales

TIMBALLETTI DI RISO ALLO ZAFFERANO

SERVES 6

¼ cup butter, melted

4 tablespoons Italian-Style Bread Crumbs (see page 230)

1½ cups short-grain white rice, such as Arborio

¼ teaspoon saffron threads or ground turmeric

½ cup freshly grated Parmesan cheese

1 egg, lightly beaten

2 tablespoons milk

½ teaspoon salt

¼ teaspoon freshly ground black pepper

These wonderful little treats make a perfect accompaniment to your favorite meat, fish, or fowl recipe.

Preheat oven to 425°.

Generously brush 6 4-ounce ramekins with the butter. Spoon 1 tablespoon of the bread crumbs into a ramekin and roll the crumbs around until they thoroughly coat the bottom and sides. Tap out the excess crumbs into the next ramekin and repeat, adding more crumbs as needed until all the ramekins are coated. Reserve the extra crumbs.

Bring 6 cups of water to a boil in a large pot over high heat. Cook the rice and saffron for 12 minutes, or until the rice is just al dente–firm, slightly undercooked. Drain the rice well, in a strainer or a colander lined with cheesecloth. In a large bowl, combine the rice, any remaining melted butter, cheese, egg, milk, salt, and pepper; stir well to incorporate. Spoon evenly into the prepared ramekins and gently press down with the back of a spoon. Sprinkle with any remaining bread crumbs. Bake for 20 to 25 minutes, until the timbales are golden brown and have started to pull away from the sides of the ramekins. Remove from oven and cool slightly before serving.

Chef's Tip

This dish is an interesting appetizer served with any of the non-dessert sauces in the Basics section. Try it first with Roasted Garlic Sauce (page 253); you won't be disappointed.

Nonna Adele

As a child, I always looked forward to spending time with my grandmother Adele, who lived near Venice. Sometimes it was even more fun than hanging around with my own friends. Nonna Adele's kitchen was a magical place—a refuge from the outside world, filled not only with wonderful smells, colors, and sounds but also with a sense of wonder for a young and impressionable boy. As she guided me through the joys of cooking, she enthralled me with stories about her own youth. In her Venetian dialect, she told me of the time during the Second World War when bombs fell on the very cornfields we could see from her window. She would shepherd her children—my mother and her brothers and sisters—into the cellar, where she entertained them with stories about beautiful princesses, handsome princes, and evil dragons.

For Nonna Adele, even an everyday occurrence was the stuff of which legends were made. As olive oil bubbled in the pan, she would recount the passionate tale of the love of the beautiful tomato for the garlic, a love blessed by the fresh basil and celebrated by the song of the sweet onions. This perfect union became the marinara sauce that graced the family table.

As the world around me changed, Nonna Adele remained one constant. And yet, after so many years of my living far from her, the memories of those days spent by her side in the kitchen are still vivid.

When I first took my American wife, Nanci, to meet Nonna Adele, it was not without anxiety. I wanted Nanci to embrace the people and places I held dear. And I hoped that my family, and Nonna Adele especially, would take Nanci into their hearts as I had done. But these were two worlds separated not just by thousands of miles but by thousands of years of traditions and expectations as well.

When we arrived at my grandmother's house in the early afternoon, she had, of course, already laid out a spread with my favorite dishes. We didn't even take the bags out of the car—we went straight to the dining room. Everything was as I remembered—the chipped crockery, the well-worn silverware, the polished wooden table, the windows overlooking the cornfields—yet it also seemed smaller.

Nonna Adele was quiet at first, busily passing food around, making sure everyone was fed. I dove into my plate with the abandon of a six-year-old who hadn't eaten in a week. Nanci was more hesitant, not knowing what was expected of her and, more important, what she should say, since my grandmother did not speak a word of English and Nanci's Italian was virtually nonexistent. Nanci realized that her few words of high school Spanish would do her little good now, and I have to admit, with my face full of pasta, I wasn't much use as a translator.

What little conversation there was, then, proceeded in fits and starts. But the wine was plentiful, and the dishes of pasta, sausages, polenta, and *crespelle* that came flowing from the magical kitchen transported me. Whatever anxiety I may have been feeling melted away. It was not long until, more than filled to satisfaction, I begged to be excused for a nap. Nonna Adele ruffled the top of my hair and kissed me on both cheeks. Nanci told me she would stay to help clean up.

When I awakened sometime later, I was vaguely aware that the better part of the afternoon had passed, but what struck me most clearly was the sound of laughter coming from below. In a daze I made my way downstairs. I could hear their voices, like schoolgirls': Nonna's singsong dialect and Nanci's halting Spanish-English. There were long moments of silence, a few words, then bursts of laughter.

When I came to the door, they both looked up from the table where, strewn before them, were piles of photographs—mostly, I soon saw, of me as a child. They were sipping wine from tumblers, their eyes glistening with tears of laughter—or perhaps a little too much *vino rosso*.

They looked at me, then back to the photographs, and once again burst into laughter. Even in my post-nap stupor it didn't take much for me to guess that I was the object of their mirth. I couldn't be sure, though, whether it was my sleepy state, hair askew, and face wrinkled by the pillow or the idea that the chubby boy in the photos was the same hulking man filling the doorway that was making them laugh more.

In some mysterious way, through this crazy collection of pictures, these two women had connected. To Nonna Adele, I would always be little Nicolino peering from the fading black-and-white images. For Nanci, here was a link to my past and to my family. Maybe it was the food or maybe it was the wine or maybe it was magic: parts of my life, and my heart, had come together in that small kitchen in my grand-mother's house in a rural Italian village thousands of miles from the place I now called home.

Pasta

Baked Pasta with Four Cheeses

Spinach Cannelloni

Crêpe Lasagna

Don Vincenzo's Rice and Lobster Timbale

Pasta with Broccoli

Pasta with Cauliflower and Garlic

Pasta with Curry Sauce

Pasta with Fennel Sauce

Pasta with Garlic and Zucchini Sauce

Pasta with Lentils and Pancetta

Pasta with Peas and Pancetta

Pasta with Peas and Tuna

Pasta with Prosciutto, Spinach, and Garbanzo Beans

Pasta with Gorgonzola and Walnut Sauce

Pasta with Salami and Rosemary Sauce

Pasta with Sausage and Pumpkin Sauce

Pasta with Sausage and Mushrooms

Pasta with Shrimp and Artichokes

Pasta with Black Squid Sauce

Pasta with Chicken, Sun-Dried Tomatoes, and Pine Nuts

Pasta with Swordfish, Lemon, and Capers

Shrimp Fritters with Roasted Garlic Sauce

Corn, Zucchini, and Pepper Soup (right)

Scallops with Prosciutto and Morels

Crêpe Lasagna

Baked Pasta with Four Cheeses

PASTA AL FORNO AI QUATTRO FORMAGGI

SERVES 6

1 tablespoon salt (optional)
Butter to grease casserole pan generously
⅜ cup Italian-Style Bread Crumbs (see page 230)
2 tablespoons olive oil
5 large cloves garlic, thickly sliced
½ teaspoon red pepper flakes
½ cup diced white onion
6 ounces prosciutto or ham, diced
1 to 1¼ pounds broccoli, thick stalks removed, cut into bite-size florets
¼ teaspoon salt (optional)
¼ teaspoon freshly ground black pepper (optional)
2 cups Chicken Stock (see page 231)
1½ cups heavy cream
2 tablespoons flour and 1½ tablespoons melted butter, mixed into a paste
1 pound orecchiette or penne rigate
4 ounces Gorgonzola cheese, cut into small chunks
4 ounces Swiss cheese, shredded or coarsely grated
4 ounces provolone cheese, cut into ¼-inch dice
½ cup freshly grated Parmesan cheese
¼ cup chopped fresh parsley

Preheat oven to 350°. Bring a large pot of water, with the salt added if desired, to a boil over high heat.

Here is my mother's version of macaroni and cheese. It is one more testimonial to her ingenuity: notice how she managed to slip in the broccoli. My brother and I liked this so much that we never noticed it.

Grease a 10x12- or 9x13-inch casserole pan well with butter. Sprinkle with ¼ cup of the bread crumbs and spread around the pan as you would flour a cake pan. Shake off excess crumbs.

In a large, deep sauté pan, heat the olive oil over medium-high heat. Add the garlic, red pepper flakes, onion, prosciutto, and broccoli. Sauté for about 5 minutes. Add the salt and pepper if desired, and stir for 1 minute. Add the stock and cream, and bring to a boil. Reduce heat and simmer, stirring occasionally, until the broccoli becomes fork-tender, about 5 minutes. Remove the broccoli with a slotted spoon and set aside.

Whisk the flour-butter paste into the sauté pan. Continue whisking on a low simmer until the sauce just begins to thicken and reduce slightly, about 8 minutes. The sauce will still be fairly liquid.

While the sauce is simmering, add the pasta to the boiling water and cook for a few minutes less than directed on the package (the pasta will continue to cook later in the oven). Drain.

When the sauce in the sauté pan is ready, add the cooked broccoli and pasta. Toss well and simmer over low heat, stirring constantly, until the pasta is well coated, about 1 to 2 minutes. Pour the contents of the pan into a large metal mixing bowl. Add the Gorgonzola, Swiss, and pro-volone cheeses and ¼ cup of the Parmesan, and the parsley. Mix well to incorporate, and pour into the prepared casserole. Sprinkle the remaining ⅛ cup bread crumbs and ¼ cup Parmesan evenly on top. Bake for 10 minutes, and broil for 2 minutes to brown the top.

Chef's Tip

Always read the package instructions before you put pasta into boiling water. Cooking times for pasta differ according to brand and type and shape. Cappellini (a.k.a. angel hair), for example, cooks a lot faster than spaghetti or penne. Fresh pasta cooks faster than dry. Italians in general prefer pasta cooked al dente, that is, firm "to the tooth," or slightly undercooked.

Spinach Cannelloni

CANNELLONI DI SPINACI

SERVES 6

This twist on the traditional cannelloni recipe uses crêpes instead of pasta. It's a lot easier to make than with fresh pasta, and once you've made it the first time you will see the endless possibilities.

3 tablespoons olive oil

1 cup chopped onion

⅓ cup chopped sun-dried tomatoes packed in olive oil, drained

6 cloves garlic, thickly sliced

¼ teaspoon red pepper flakes

1 pound fresh spinach, washed, rinsed, and dried, thick stems removed

15 ounces ricotta cheese

1 egg, lightly beaten

1 recipe Parmesan Béchamel Sauce (see page 243)

½ cup freshly grated Romano cheese

½ cup plus 2 tablespoons freshly grated Parmesan cheese

1 teaspoon salt

½ teaspoon freshly ground black pepper

1 recipe Savory Crêpes (see page 272)

2 cups Tomato Sauce (see page 235), or 1 14.5-ounce can stewed Italian-style tomatoes, pureed

1 tablespoon chopped fresh Italian parsley

Preheat oven to 375°.

In a large sauté pan, heat the olive oil over medium heat. Add the onion, sun-dried tomatoes, garlic, and red pepper flakes until the onion is tender, about 6 minutes. Add the spinach and cook until wilted and dry, 6 to 8 minutes. Let cool.

In a large bowl, blend the ricotta, egg, and ¾ cup of the Parmesan Béchamel Sauce. Add the spinach mixture, Romano cheese, the ½ cup Parmesan, salt, and pepper and stir to combine.

Make the Savory Crêpes.

Lightly grease a large lasagna pan with olive oil and pour the tomato sauce in the bottom. Place ½ cup of the spinach mixture in the middle of each crêpe and roll each up like a fat cigar. Place the filled crêpes/cannelloni on the tomato sauce in the lasagna pan. Pour the remaining béchamel sauce on top. Sprinkle with the 2 tablespoons Parmesan and the parsley, and bake for 25 to 30 minutes, or until the crêpes/cannelloni are warmed through and the sauce is lightly brown and bubbly. Let cool for 10 minutes before serving.

Crêpe Lasagna

LASAGNE DI CRESPELLE

SERVES 6 GENEROUSLY

2 recipes Savory Crêpes (see page 272)
1 recipe Meat Sauce (see page 240)
1 recipe Parmesan Béchamel Sauce (see page 243)
⅛ teaspoon freshly grated nutmeg
1 cup freshly grated Parmesan cheese
1 tablespoon chopped fresh Italian parsley

*M*ore commonly known as crêpes, crespelle *are as versatile as your imagination. Once you've mastered the basic technique, you'll want to use them in a wide array of sweet and savory dishes. This lasagna using crêpes instead of the usual pasta should inspire you to create your own specialties.*

Preheat oven to 375°.

Prepare the crêpes, meat sauce, and béchamel sauce. Fold the nutmeg into the béchamel sauce.

Lightly grease a lasagna pan with olive oil, and pour in 1 cup of the meat sauce. Top with a layer of crêpes and spread with a thin layer of the béchamel sauce (about ¼ cup), then sprinkle with grated cheese and top with another layer of crêpes and a thin layer of meat sauce. Repeat layering to the top of the pan, making plenty of layers; keep each layer thin. Finish with a layer of crêpes and béchamel sauce, and sprinkle with the grated cheese and parsley. Bake for 25 to 30 minutes, or until light brown and bubbly. Let rest for at least 10 minutes before serving.

Don Vincenzo's Rice and Lobster Timbale

SFORMATO DI RISO E ARAGOSTA DON VINCENZO

SERVES 6 TO 8

7 small lobster tails, steamed (about 2 pounds)
3 cups Lobster Sauce (see page 250)
6 cups Arborio rice
15 tablespoons butter
¼ tightly packed cup chopped fresh parsley
2 small eggs
1½ cups freshly grated Parmesan cheese
½ cup Italian-Style Bread Crumbs (see page 230)
¼ teaspoon curry
4 tablespoons brandy

This recipe was always part of a traditional holiday menu in the Stellino house.

Remove the lobster meat from the shells. Use the shells to make the Lobster Sauce; prepare it before you do anything else.

Preheat oven to 350°.

Trim ¼ inch from each end of the lobster tails and discard. Cut the tails in half, and slice in ¼-inch pieces. Place in a covered bowl in the refrigerator.

Bring a large pot of water to a boil over high heat. Add the rice and cook for 8 to 10 minutes, until al dente, or slightly crunchy. Drain and remove to a large bowl. Add 6 tablespoons of the butter, parsley, eggs,

1 cup Lobster Sauce, and Parmesan. Stir well to incorporate all the ingredients, cover, and set aside.

Grease a 9x5x3-inch ovenproof glass loaf pan with 1 tablespoon of the butter, and coat with the bread crumbs as you would flour a cake pan. Shake off excess crumbs. Fill the pan with the rice mixture and bake for 20 minutes.

In a large, deep skillet, heat 4 tablespoons of the butter over medium heat until sizzling, about 3 minutes. Add the lobster meat and curry, and cook for 3 to 4 minutes, stirring well. Add the brandy and cook for 3 minutes. Remove the lobster to a bowl with a slotted spoon, and cover with aluminum foil to keep warm.

Pour the remaining 2 cups Lobster Sauce into the skillet and bring to a boil. Reduce to a simmer and cook for 7 to 8 minutes. Add the lobster and reheat for 2 minutes, stirring well.

Remove the loaf pan from the oven and invert over a platter. The rice mixture should slide out holding the shape of the pan, and the bread crumbs should have baked to a golden crust. While the sauce is still cooking, remove the lobster pieces from the skillet with a slotted spoon. Place them on top of and around the rice loaf.

Turn off heat under the skillet and add the remaining 4 tablespoons butter to the sauce, stirring well to incorporate. Pour half of the sauce over the rice loaf, and put the other half in a gravy boat. Bring to the table and serve with pride.

Chef's Tip

This magnificent dish can be served in various ways, to suit various occasions. For a more formal presentation you might want to bake the rice in individual ramekins, each decorated with the lobster and sauce. You could also make the timbale in a Bundt or other ring cake pan, and arrange the lobster and sauce in the hole in the middle.

Pasta with Broccoli

PASTA AL SUGO DI BROCCOLI

SERVES 6

In Sicilian cuisine, the marriage of broccoli and garlic is a common yet super-lative combination. Each ingredient raises the other to heights of culinary majesty.

1 tablespoon salt (optional)

1 ½ pounds broccoli, thick stalks removed, cut into bite-size florets

3 tablespoons olive oil

¼ teaspoon red pepper flakes

4 cloves garlic, thickly sliced

5 to 6 ounces prosciutto or ham, roughly chopped

¼ teaspoon salt

¼ teaspoon freshly ground black pepper

1 ¾ cups Chicken Stock (see page 231) or canned vegetable stock

1 pound fusilli or penne rigate

¾ cup freshly grated Romano cheese

Bring a large pot of water, with 1 tablespoon salt added if desired, to a boil over high heat. Add broccoli and blanch for 1 to 2 minutes. Remove with a slotted spoon to a bowl of ice water to stop the cooking. Drain well and set aside. Keep the pot of water boiling.

In a large, deep sauté pan, heat the olive oil over medium-high heat. Add the red pepper flakes and garlic, and sauté for 1 minute. Add the prosciutto and broccoli. Do not toss. Allow the broccoli to sit on the heat for 3 to 4 minutes, then turn gently and allow the other side to sit on the heat for the same amount of time. Season with the ¼ teaspoon salt and the pepper.

Deglaze the pan with the stock. Bring to a boil, then reduce heat and simmer for 10 to 15 minutes.

While the sauce is simmering, cook the pasta in the boiling broccoli water according to the directions on the package. Drain and return to the pot. Pour the broccoli sauce over the pasta and simmer over low heat, stirring constantly so that the pasta is well coated, for about 3 minutes. Remove from heat. Add the cheese, toss gently, and serve.

Pasta with Cauliflower and Garlic

PASTA CON CAVOLFIORE E AGLIO

SERVES 6

This dish and its variations are very popular in southern Italy. My father often asked my mother to make it because it reminded him of being a child at his father's table. I suspect that long after my grandfather Don Nicola had passed away, this dish had become a symbol of the best moments my father and his father had spent together.

1 tablespoon salt (optional)

1 ½ pounds head cauliflower, cut into florets

3 tablespoons olive oil

4 large cloves garlic, thickly sliced

½ teaspoon red pepper flakes

½ large white onion, cut in half lengthwise and thinly sliced

½ teaspoon salt

¼ teaspoon freshly ground black pepper

2 teaspoons anchovy paste

¾ cup chopped fresh parsley

1 ¾ cups Chicken Stock (see page 231) or canned vegetable stock

1 pound orecchiette or penne rigate

½ cup freshly grated Romano cheese

Bring a large pot of water, with the 1 tablespoon salt added if desired, to a boil over high heat. Add the cauliflower. Cook for 2 to 3 minutes. Remove with a slotted spoon into a bowl of ice water to stop the cooking. Drain well and set aside. Keep the pot of water boiling.

In a large, deep sauté pan, heat the olive oil over medium heat. Add the garlic, red pepper flakes, and onion. Cook for 2 minutes, until well coated with oil. Add the cauliflower and cook for 8 to 10 minutes, or until onion and cauliflower begin to brown lightly. Stir after 4 minutes. Season with the ½ teaspoon salt and the pepper.

In a small bowl, mix the anchovy paste with 1 tablespoon of the water used to cook the cauliflower. Add ½ cup of the parsley to the cauliflower mixture. Add the stock. Bring to a boil, then reduce heat and simmer to a saucelike consistency, about 15 to 18 minutes.

While the sauce is simmering, cook the pasta in the boiling cauliflower water according to the directions on the package. Drain and return to the pot. Pour the sauce over the pasta and simmer over low heat, stirring constantly so that the pasta is well coated, for about 2 minutes. Remove from heat. Add the cheese and stir well. Sprinkle with the remaining ¼ cup parsley and serve.

Pasta with Curry Sauce

PASTA AL SUGO DI CURRY

SERVES 6

1 tablespoon salt (optional)

3 tablespoons unsalted butter

½ cup diced white onion

6 ounces honey-glazed ham, cut into ¼-inch dice (about 1 cup)

1 medium Granny Smith apple, peeled, cored, and cut in ½-inch dice
    (1 ¼ to 1 ½ cups)

½ teaspoon curry powder

¼ teaspoon freshly ground black pepper

¼ cup brandy

½ cup heavy cream

1 ¼ cups Chicken Stock (see page 231)

1 cup frozen peas

4 ounces Gorgonzola cheese, crumbled or cut into small pieces

Salt and pepper to taste

1 pound fettuccine or linguine

½ cup freshly grated Parmesan cheese

My father came up with this recipe after a trip he and my mother took to France, where apples seemed to appear in one form or another at every meal. It was a while before he perfected it—my brother and I have plenty of stories about that. This dish is a perfect example of successful culinary improvisation: though the combination of ingredients is unusual, the result is one of unparalleled flavor.

Bring a large pot of water, with the 1 tablespoon salt added if desired, to a boil over high heat.

In a large, deep sauté pan, melt the butter over medium heat. Add the onion and ham, and sauté for 2 minutes. Add the apple, curry, and pepper. Toss well and sauté for 2 minutes.

Deglaze the pan with the brandy. Cook until liquid is reduced by half, 2 to 3 minutes. Add the cream, stock, and frozen peas. Bring to a boil.

Add the Gorgonzola and stir well. Reduce heat and simmer for about 15 minutes. Taste for salt and pepper and season as desired.

While the sauce is simmering, cook the pasta in the boiling water according to the directions on the package. Drain and return to the pot. Pour the sauce over the pasta. Simmer over low heat, stirring constantly so that the pasta is well coated, for about 3 minutes. Remove from heat. Add the Parmesan and stir well, and serve.

Pasta with Fennel Sauce

PASTA AL SUGO DI FINOCCHIO

SERVES 6 GENEROUSLY

Fennel, that anise-flavored bulb, is a favorite of Sicilian chefs. Here it adds a subtle yet distinctive flavor to a rich, smooth sauce.

1 tablespoon salt (optional)
1 bulb fennel
4 tablespoons olive oil
1 cup thinly sliced onion
½ cup pine nuts
6 cloves garlic, thickly sliced
⅛ teaspoon red pepper flakes
2 teaspoons grated lemon zest
2 tablespoons chopped fresh Italian parsley
½ cup white wine
1 cup heavy cream
1 cup Chicken Stock (see page 231) or canned vegetable stock
1 teaspoon salt
½ teaspoon freshly ground black pepper
1 pound linguine, penne rigate, or spaghetti
6 tablespoons freshly grated Parmesan cheese

Bring a large pot of water, with the 1 tablespoon salt added if desired, to a boil over high heat.

Trim away the tough green stalks of the fennel, and scrape or cut away any brown spots. Slice the bulb in half lengthwise and remove the inner core. Slice the remaining bulb into matchstick-size pieces.

In a sauté pan, heat the olive oil over medium heat. Add the fennel and onion until they soften slightly, 2 to 3 minutes. Stir in the pine nuts, garlic, red pepper flakes, lemon zest, and 1 tablespoon of the parsley. Sauté, stirring regularly until the garlic and pine nuts start to brown, 6 to 8 minutes.

Deglaze the pan with the wine, stirring to dislodge any browned bits from the bottom of the pan, and continue cooking to reduce liquid by half. Add the cream, stock, the 1 teaspoon salt, and the pepper, and simmer for 10 to 12 minutes, or until the sauce has thickened and coats the back of a wooden spoon.

Cook the pasta in the boiling water according to the directions on the package. Drain and return to the pot. Pour the sauce over the pasta and simmer over low heat, stirring constantly so that the pasta is well coated, for about 3 minutes. Remove from heat. Add the Parmesan, stir well, and serve.

Pasta with Garlic and Zucchini Sauce

PASTA CON "RAGÙ" DI ZUCCHINE

SERVES 6

This humble dish has an explosive flavor which I like to say seduces the unwitting diner into culinary ecstasy.

1 tablespoon salt (optional)

5 tablespoons olive oil

6 medium zucchini, cut into ½-inch dice

6 cloves garlic, thickly sliced

3 tablespoons chopped fresh basil, or 1 tablespoon dried

1½ tablespoons chopped fresh mint, or 1 teaspoon dried

½ teaspoon red pepper flakes

2 cups Chicken Stock (see page 231) or canned vegetable stock

½ teaspoon salt

½ teaspoon freshly ground black pepper

1 pound penne rigate or tortiglioni

¼ cup freshly grated Romano cheese

Bring a large pot of water, with the 1 tablespoon salt added if desired, to a boil over high heat.

In a large saucepan, heat the olive oil over medium-high heat. Add the zucchini and sauté until brown, about 6 to 8 minutes. Add the garlic, herbs, and red pepper flakes, and stir well. Sauté for 3 to 4 minutes, or until the garlic starts to brown.

Add the stock, stirring well to deglaze the pan and dislodge any browned bits from the bottom. Bring to a boil, and simmer until the mixture reaches a saucelike consistency, about 10 to 12 minutes. Add the ½ teaspoon each salt and pepper.

Cook the pasta in the boiling water according to the directions on the package. Drain and return to the pot. Pour the sauce over the pasta, simmer over low heat, stirring constantly so that the pasta is well coated, for about 3 minutes. Remove from heat. Add the cheese, stir well, and serve.

Pasta with Lentils and Pancetta

PASTA CON LENTICCHIE E PANCETTA

SERVES 6

In this dish, typical to southern Italy, the combination of ingredients creates an explosion of flavor. Enjoy it with a glass of red wine, and imagine you are looking at the rolling hills of the Sicilian countryside.

1 tablespoon salt (optional)

3 tablespoons olive oil

¼ teaspoon red pepper flakes

4 large cloves garlic, thickly sliced

4 ounces pancetta or bacon, cut into ¼-inch dice

½ cup finely diced carrot (1 medium)

½ cup finely diced celery (1½ stalks)

½ cup finely diced onion

¾ cup white wine

1 28-ounce can Italian-style peeled tomatoes, drained and chopped, juice reserved

10 fresh basil leaves, rolled like cigarettes and thinly sliced, plus 6 small leaves for garnish

1 teaspoon dried thyme

½ teaspoon sugar

¼ teaspoon salt

2½ cups Chicken Stock (see page 231)

¾ cup dried lentils, rinsed, picked over, and drained

Salt and pepper to taste

1 pound fusilli, orecchiette, penne rigate, or tortiglioni

6 tablespoons freshly grated Romano cheese

Bring a large pot of water, with the 1 tablespoon salt added if desired, to a boil over high heat.

In a large, deep sauté pan, heat the olive oil over medium-high heat. Add the red pepper flakes and garlic, and sauté until the garlic turns a light brown, 2 to 3 minutes. Add the pancetta and sauté for 1 minute. Add the carrot, celery, and onion, and sauté until the onion is very soft, about 8 to 10 minutes.

Deglaze the pan with the wine, and continue cooking to reduce liquid by a third, about 5 to 7 minutes. Add the tomatoes, sliced basil leaves, thyme, sugar, and the ¼ teaspoon salt. Cook for 2 to 3 minutes. Add the stock and reserved tomato juice. Bring to a boil.

Reduce heat, then add the lentils and simmer for about 25 to 30 minutes. The sauce will thicken as the lentils cook and absorb liquid. Check them after 20 minutes—you do not want them to get mushy. They should be al dente, cooked through but firm. Season with salt and pepper as desired.

Cook the pasta in the boiling water according to the directions on the package. Drain and return to the pot. Pour the sauce over the pasta, and simmer over low heat, stirring constantly until the pasta is well coated, for about 3 minutes. Turn off heat, add the cheese, and stir well. Garnish with the basil leaves and serve.

Pasta with Peas and Pancetta

PASTA CON PISELLI E PANCETTA

Next time you're looking for a simple but interesting recipe, full of flavor, try this jewel.

SERVES 6 GENEROUSLY

1 tablespoon salt (optional)

1 small carrot

1 stalk celery

½ medium onion

3 tablespoons olive oil

6 ounces pancetta or bacon, chopped

6 cloves garlic, thickly sliced

¼ cup chopped fresh basil

2 tablespoons chopped fresh Italian parsley

¼ teaspoon red pepper flakes

1 28-ounce can Italian-style peeled tomatoes, drained and chopped,
    juice reserved

1 cup white wine

½ teaspoon salt

¼ teaspoon freshly ground black pepper

1 cup fresh or frozen peas

1 pound penne rigate or spaghetti

6 tablespoons freshly grated Romano cheese

Bring a large pot of water, with the 1 tablespoon salt added if desired, to a boil over high heat.

Make a mirepoix—a flavorful vegetable base—with the carrot, celery, and onion by finely chopping or whirling them in a food processor until just blended, 10 to 12 quick pulses. In a large, deep sauté pan, heat the olive oil over medium heat. Add the pancetta, and sauté until it starts to brown, 2 to 3 minutes. Add the prepared mirepoix, garlic, basil, parsley, and red pepper flakes, and sauté until the vegetables are tender, about 3 to 4 minutes. Stir in the tomatoes, and cook until their water has evaporated, about 7 minutes. Deglaze the pan with the wine, and continue cooking to reduce liquid by half. Add the reserved tomato juice, the ½ teaspoon salt, and pepper, and bring to a boil. Simmer until thickened to a saucelike consistency, 10 to 12 minutes. Stir in the peas and cook until tender, 3 to 5 minutes.

Cook the pasta in the boiling water according to the directions on the package. Drain and return to the pot. Pour the sauce over the pasta and simmer over low heat, stirring constantly until the pasta is well coated, for about 3 minutes. Turn the pasta out onto a warm serving dish and sprinkle with the cheese. Serve immediately.

Pasta with Peas and Tuna

PASTA CON PISELLI E TONNO

This recipe is very quick and easy to make. The humble canned tuna rises to the occasion and adds to a surprising complexity of flavor.

SERVES 6 GENEROUSLY

1 tablespoon salt (optional)
1 10-ounce package frozen peas
4 tablespoons olive oil
1 cup chopped onion
6 cloves garlic, thickly sliced
¼ teaspoon red pepper flakes
2 tablespoons chopped fresh Italian parsley
2 6-ounce cans solid white albacore tuna packed in water, drained
1 tablespoon grated lemon zest
2 cups clam juice or Chicken Stock (see page 231)
¼ cup freshly squeezed lemon juice
¼ teaspoon salt
¼ teaspoon freshly ground black pepper
1 pound linguine or spaghetti

Bring a large pot of water, with the 1 tablespoon salt added if desired, to a boil over high heat.

Rinse the peas under warm water for a few seconds and drain well.

In a large sauté pan, heat the olive oil over medium heat until sizzling. Sauté the onion, garlic, red pepper flakes, and 1 tablespoon of the parsley until the onion is lightly colored, about 6 to 7 minutes. Stir in the tuna and lemon zest, breaking the tuna into flakes. Add the clam juice or stock, lemon juice, the ¼ teaspoon salt, and pepper. Bring to a boil, then simmer to a saucelike consistency for about 8 to 10 minutes. Stir in the peas and cook for 2 minutes.

Cook the pasta according to the directions on the package. Drain and return to the pot. Pour the sauce over the pasta and simmer over low heat, stirring constantly until the pasta is well coated, for about 3 minutes. Remove from heat, sprinkle with the remaining 1 tablespoon parsley, and serve.

Pasta with Prosciutto, Spinach, and Garbanzo Beans

PASTA ALLA CONTADINA

SERVES 6

This rustic dish delivers an unexpected note of sophistication with the spinach cream. It is unusual in its preparation, yet the mingling of flavors is typical of Italian country cooking.

1 tablespoon salt (optional)

6 tablespoons olive oil

1 10-ounce package fresh spinach, washed, rinsed, and dried, thick stems removed

½ teaspoon salt

¼ teaspoon freshly ground black pepper

1¾ cups Chicken Stock (see page 231)

3 large cloves garlic, thickly sliced

1 cup chopped white onion

¼ teaspoon red pepper flakes

8 ounces prosciutto or ham, finely chopped

1 14.5-ounce can garbanzo beans, drained

¼ cup chopped fresh parsley

¼ cup chopped fresh basil

¾ cup white wine

½ cup heavy cream

3 medium tomatoes, seeded and diced, tossed with 1 tablespoon olive oil and pinch of salt and pepper

1 pound fusilli or penne rigate

½ cup freshly grated Parmesan cheese

Bring a large pot of water, with the 1 tablespoon salt added if desired, to a boil over high heat.

In a large, deep sauté pan, heat 2 tablespoons of the olive oil over medium-high heat. Add the spinach, season with the salt and pepper, and sauté until wilted. Add ¼ cup of the stock. Bring to a boil, and reduce liquid by half. Let cool, then place the mixture in a blender and puree well. Set aside.

In the same sauté pan, heat the remaining 4 tablespoons olive oil over medium-high heat. Add the garlic, onion, red pepper flakes, prosciutto, garbanzo beans, parsley, and basil. Cook until the onion is softened, about 4 to 6 minutes. Deglaze the pan with the wine, and continue cooking to reduce liquid by half.

Add the spinach mixture, the remaining 1½ cups stock, and cream. Stir well. Bring to a boil, then simmer for about 10 minutes. Add the tomatoes and simmer for 5 minutes.

While the sauce is simmering, cook the pasta in the boiling water according to the directions on the package. Drain and return to the pot. When the sauce is ready, pour over the pasta and simmer over low heat, stirring constantly until the pasta is well coated, for about 2 minutes. Add the cheese, toss gently, and serve.

Pasta with Gorgonzola and Walnut Sauce

PASTA AL SUGO DI NOCI E GORGONZOLA

SERVES 6 GENEROUSLY

Walnuts, prosciutto, and Gorgonzola here create a wonderful symphony of flavors. These flavors are traditional in northern Italian cooking, but for those of us who love to eat, that makes very little difference: this foolproof recipe tastes great wherever it comes from.

1 tablespoon salt (optional)
¾ cup walnut halves or pieces
½ cup heavy cream, warmed
2 tablespoons butter
2 tablespoons olive oil
1 cup chopped onion
4 ounces prosciutto or ham, finely chopped (½ cup)
4 cloves garlic, thickly sliced
¼ teaspoon red pepper flakes
1 cup sparkling white wine or Champagne
1 cup Chicken Stock (see page 231)
½ teaspoon salt
¼ teaspoon freshly ground black pepper
½ cup crumbled Gorgonzola cheese
¼ cup freshly grated Parmesan cheese
1 tablespoon chopped fresh Italian parsley
1 pound conchiglie, farfalle, fusilli, or penne rigate

Bring a large pot of water, with the 1 tablespoon salt added if desired, to a boil over high heat.

Puree ½ cup of the walnuts and the cream in a food processor or blender until smooth. Set aside the remaining walnuts.

In a large sauté pan, melt the butter with the olive oil over medium heat until bubbling. Sauté the onion, prosciutto, garlic, and red pepper flakes until the onion is tender and the prosciutto begins to brown, 6 to 8 minutes. Deglaze the pan with the wine, stirring to dislodge any browned bits from the bottom of the pan. Continue cooking to reduce liquid by half. Stir in the stock, walnut puree, the ½ teaspoon salt, and pepper. Bring to a boil, then simmer to a saucelike consistency for 10 to 12 minutes. Melt the Gorgonzola and Parmesan cheeses in the sauce.

Cook the pasta in the boiling water according to the directions on the package. Drain and return to the pot. Pour the sauce over the pasta, and simmer over low heat, stirring constantly until the pasta is well coated, for about 3 minutes.

Turn the pasta out onto a warm serving dish, sprinkle with the parsley and remaining ¼ cup walnuts, and serve.

Pasta with Salami and Rosemary Sauce

PASTA AL SUGO DI ROSMARINO E SALAME

SERVES 6

The aggressive combination of salami and rosemary is representative of the flavors used in Sicilian and southern Italian cooking.

1 tablespoon salt (optional)

4 tablespoons olive oil

4 cloves garlic, thickly sliced

½ cup chopped white onion

8 ounces salami, very finely chopped (soppressata or salame toscano is best)

¼ cup chopped fresh parsley, plus 2 tablespoons for garnish

4 teaspoons finely chopped fresh rosemary, or 1 heaping teaspoon dried, crushed between fingers before use

2 loosely packed tablespoons finely sliced fresh basil (10 to 12 leaves), or 1½ teaspoons dried

1 teaspoon finely sliced fresh sage (3 leaves), or ¼ teaspoon dried

¼ teaspoon freshly ground black pepper

¾ cup red wine

1 cup canned tomato sauce

¾ cup Chicken Stock (see page 231)

½ cup finely diced Romano cheese

1 pound corkscrew pasta, farfalle, fusilli, orecchiette, or penne rigate

Bring a large pot of water, with the 1 tablespoon salt added if desired, to a boil over high heat.

In a large, deep sauté pan, heat the olive oil over medium-high heat. Add the garlic and sauté for 2 minutes. Add the onion and sauté for 3 to 4 minutes. Add the salami and the herbs (except the 2 tablespoons parsley for garnish). Sauté until the onion is soft and the garlic is browned, about 5 to 7 minutes. Season with the pepper (the salami is salty, so you won't need to add salt).

Add the wine, stirring well to dislodge any browned bits from the bottom of the pan. Continue cooking to reduce liquid by half, about 2 to 3 minutes. Add the tomato sauce and stock. Bring to a boil, then simmer for 10 to 12 minutes.

While the sauce is simmering, cook the pasta in the boiling water according to the directions on the package. Drain well and return to the pot. Pour the sauce over the pasta, and simmer over low heat, stirring constantly, for 2 to 3 minutes. Turn off heat and add the cheese, stir well for 2 minutes, and serve.

Pasta with Sausage and Pumpkin Sauce

PASTA AL SUGO DI ZUCCA E SALSICCIA

SERVES 6 TO 8

This is the perfect dish to warm you up on a crisp evening and celebrate the glory of autumn.

4 tablespoons olive oil
1 pound spicy Italian sausage, casing removed
1 cup chopped onion
10 cloves garlic, thickly sliced
3 tablespoons chopped fresh sage
¼ teaspoon red pepper flakes (optional)
1 ¼ cups white wine
1 ¼ cups canned pumpkin puree
2 cups Chicken Stock (see page 231)
¼ teaspoon cinnamon (optional)
Salt and pepper to taste
1 tablespoon salt (optional)
1 pound penne, penne rigate, rigatoni, or tortiglioni
6 tablespoons freshly grated Parmesan cheese (optional)

In a large, deep sauté pan, heat 1 tablespoon of the olive oil over high heat for 2 minutes. Add the sausage, and cook until brown, about 3 minutes. While it browns, break it up into bite-size pieces with the back of a wooden spoon. Turn off heat, and remove the sausage to a bowl with a slotted spoon. Cover and set aside.

Keep 1 tablespoon of the oil in the pan, and discard the rest. Add the remaining 3 tablespoons olive oil, and cook over medium heat for 3 minutes. Add the onion, garlic, and sage, and cook for 10 minutes, stirring well, until the onion and garlic start to brown. (If you like things spicy, sprinkle in the red pepper flakes now.) Add the sausage and cook for 2 minutes, stirring well. Deglaze the pan with the wine and cook for 8 minutes, stirring well to dislodge any browned bits from the bottom of the pan.

Add the pumpkin puree and cook for 2 minutes, stirring well. Add the stock (and cinnamon if desired), bring to a boil over high heat, then reduce heat and simmer for 30 minutes. Add salt and pepper to taste.

While the sauce is cooking, bring a large pot of water, with the 1 tablespoon salt added if desired, to a boil over high heat. Add the pasta and cook according to the instructions on the package. Drain well in a colander over the sink and pour back into the pot. Add the sauce and cook over medium heat for 3 to 5 minutes, stirring constantly. Remove from heat, add the Parmesan if desired, and serve.

Pasta with Sausage and Mushrooms

PASTA CON SALSICCIA E FUNGHI

SERVES 6

Legend has it that Don Calogero La Mantia, food critic for a small paper in the town of Terrasini, responded thus to his doctor's concerns about his overeating: "Heaven can wait, at least until I finish one more plate of this pasta."

1 tablespoon salt (optional)

4 tablespoons olive oil

1 pound spicy Italian sausage, casing removed

⅛ teaspoon red pepper flakes

4 large cloves garlic, thickly sliced

½ cup chopped onion

½ teaspoon salt

¼ teaspoon freshly ground black pepper

½ teaspoon chopped fresh sage

½ teaspoon chopped fresh rosemary

1 pound small cremini or white button mushrooms, brushed clean and
    stems trimmed, quartered

1 cup white wine

2 cups Chicken Stock (see page 231)

⅛ cup thinly sliced fresh basil

½ cup chopped fresh parsley

¾ cup freshly grated Parmesan cheese

1 pound corkscrew pasta, spaghetti, or tortiglioni

Bring a large pot of water, with the 1 tablespoon salt added if desired, to a boil over high heat.

In a large, deep sauté pan, heat 2 tablespoons of the olive oil over medium-high heat. Add the sausage and sauté, breaking it up into small pieces with the back of a wooden spoon. Cook until the sausage is cooked through and there is no pink color left. Remove to a bowl with a slotted spoon and set aside.

Add the red pepper flakes, garlic, onion, the ½ teaspoon salt, pepper, sage, and rosemary to the oil in the pan. Sauté over medium heat until the onion is soft, about 5 to 7 minutes. Add the remaining 2 tablespoons olive oil to the pan, and increase heat to high. Add the mushrooms and sauté, stirring constantly, until golden brown but still holding their shape, about 3 to 4 minutes. The mushrooms will absorb the oil readily, so watch the pan carefully.

Return the sausage to the sauté pan, and stir to combine well. Add the wine, stirring well to dislodge any browned bits from the bottom of the pan. Bring to a boil and cook until liquid is reduced by half, 2 to 3 minutes. Add the stock, basil, and half of the parsley. Stir well, bring to a boil, then simmer for 10 to 12 minutes.

While the sauce is simmering, cook the pasta in the boiling water according to the directions on the package. Drain and return to the pot. Pour the sauce over the pasta and simmer over low heat, stirring constantly until the pasta is well coated, about 3 minutes. Remove from heat. Add ½ cup of the Parmesan, toss gently, sprinkle with the remaining parsley—and additional cheese to taste—and serve.

Pasta with Shrimp and Artichokes

PASTA CON GAMBERI E CARCIOFI

SERVES 6 GENEROUSLY

1 tablespoon salt (optional)

2 cups water

Juice of 1 lemon

4 large fresh artichokes or 1 14-ounce can artichoke bottoms, rinsed and
    drained

1½ pounds medium shrimp, peeled and deveined

½ teaspoon salt

½ teaspoon freshly ground black pepper

4 tablespoons olive oil

1 cup chopped onion

6 cloves garlic, thickly sliced

2 teaspoons grated lemon zest

⅛ teaspoon red pepper flakes

1 cup white wine

1 cup Chicken Stock (see page 231)

2 tablespoons freshly squeezed lemon juice

2 tablespoons chopped fresh Italian parsley

1 pound linguine, spaghetti, or spaghettini

½ cup diced tomato (optional)

Bring a large pot of water, with the 1 tablespoon salt added if desired,
to a boil over high heat.

If using fresh artichokes: In a small bowl, mix the 2 cups water and the
juice of the lemon. Rub the cut lemon halves on your hands to prevent
your fingers from blackening. Snap off the dark outer leaves of each artichoke by bending them back. Cut off the stem and remaining leaves

Artichokes are among the most mysterious foods. You can't precisely describe the taste, yet they have an unmistakable flavor that titillates the palate. With this dish, where they combine with shrimp, there is nothing left to do but surrender to the overwhelming power of this alliance.

at the natural curve separating the heart and the coarse tips. With a sharp paring knife, trim away the tough green skin and any remaining pieces of coarse leaves. Scoop out the thistle-like choke with a metal spoon. Drop the prepared artichoke bottom into the lemon water to prevent discoloration. Cut the artichoke bottoms into ¼-inch slices.

If using canned artichoke bottoms: Rinse and drain thoroughly before slicing.

Pat the shrimp dry and toss with ¼ teaspoon each of the salt and pepper. In a large sauté pan, heat the olive oil over medium-high heat until sizzling. Add half of the shrimp and quickly brown on both sides, about 1 minute per side. Remove the shrimp to a bowl with a slotted spoon. Brown the remaining shrimp and remove to the bowl. Decrease heat to medium-low, and in the same pan, sauté the artichoke slices, onion, garlic, lemon zest, and red pepper flakes until the artichoke slices and onion start to brown, about 10 to 12 minutes.

Add the wine and stir gently to dislodge any browned bits from the bottom of the pan. Continue to cook until liquid is reduced by half. Add the stock, lemon juice, 1 tablespoon of the parsley, and the remaining salt and pepper. Bring to a boil, then simmer until slightly thickened, about 10 minutes.

While the sauce is simmering, cook the pasta in the boiling water according to the directions on the package. Drain and return to the pot. Return the shrimp to the sauce to just warm through, no more than 2 to 3 minutes. Pour the sauce over the pasta and simmer over low heat, stirring constantly until the pasta is well coated, for about 2 minutes. Turn the pasta out onto a warm serving dish, sprinkle with the remaining parsley (and diced tomato if desired), and serve.

Pasta with Black Squid Sauce

SPAGHETTI AL SUGO NERO DI SEPPIE

SERVES 6 GENEROUSLY

My father fell in love with Naples when he was stationed there during his military service. This dish, like many others in his repertoire, was influenced by the culinary offerings of that great city. The color of the sauce might be offputting to the uninitiated, but if you don't try this dish, you'll be cheating yourself out of a great pleasure.

1 tablespoon salt (optional)
1½ pounds fresh whole squid, or 1 pound cleaned tubes and tentacles
1 cup chopped onion
¼ cup chopped fresh Italian parsley
6 cloves garlic, thickly sliced
1½ tablespoons grated lemon zest, plus extra for garnish (optional)
6 tablespoons olive oil
¼ teaspoon red pepper flakes
½ cup white wine
1 cup Tomato Sauce (see page 235)
1 cup clam juice
½ teaspoon salt
½ teaspoon freshly ground black pepper
⅛ teaspoon squid ink (see instructions and tip below)
1 pound linguine, spaghetti, or spaghettini

Bring a large pot of water, with the 1 tablespoon salt added if desired, to a boil over high heat.

If using whole squid: Rinse thoroughly. Pull the tentacles from the body sac. (To obtain the ink, remove the slender silver ink sac from the strands connected to the tentacles. Place the ink sacs in a small bowl covered with a few drops of water until ready to use. See also tip below.) Clean the tentacles by cutting just below the eyes; retain only the leg portion. Turn back the tentacles and squeeze gently to reveal the beadlike beak. Pinch off and discard. Gently squeeze out the viscera from the tubes, and remove the hard, transparent "quill" that runs the length of the interior wall. Peel the purplish skin from the outside of the tubes. Rinse and pat dry. Chop the tubes and slice the tentacles into quarters. Refrigerate until ready to use.

Make a *tritato,* a minced mixture to serve as a flavorful base for the sauce. In a food processor or with a sharp knife, chop together the onion, parsley, garlic, and lemon zest so they are fully amalgamated but not a paste.

In a large sauté pan, heat the olive oil over medium heat. Add the prepared *tritato* and red pepper flakes, and cook until onion is tender and aromatic, but not brown. Add the squid and sauté until firm and beginning to release natural juices, about 2 minutes.

Add the wine and continue to cook until liquid is reduced by half, 2 to 3 minutes. Add the Tomato Sauce, clam juice, the ½ teaspoon salt, and pepper. Bring to a boil, then simmer gently until squid is tender and sauce thickens, 10 to 12 minutes. Do not boil too quickly, or the squid will become tough and rubbery. With a skewer or the tip of a knife, blend in a few drops of squid ink at a time until the sauce is a dark, savory brown.

Cook the pasta in the boiling water according to the directions on the package. Drain and return to the pot. Pour the sauce over the pasta and simmer over low heat, stirring constantly until the pasta is well coated, for about 2 minutes. Remove from heat and serve. Garnish with extra lemon zest if desired.

Chef's Tip

If you aren't using fresh squid ink, you can find the ink at a good gourmet shop or fish market. A scant ⅛ teaspoon turns the finished sauce a dark blackish-brown without looking too inky.

Pasta with Chicken, Sun-Dried Tomatoes, and Pine Nuts

PASTA DI ZIA CICCINA

SERVES 4 TO 6

1 tablespoon salt (optional)
4 tablespoons olive oil
½ white onion, chopped
5 cloves garlic, thickly sliced
½ cup finely chopped sun-dried tomatoes packed in olive oil,
    drained before chopping
½ cup pine nuts
1 small boneless, skinless chicken breast, broiled and finely diced
    (about ¾ cup; see tip below)
¼ cup brandy
1 28-ounce can Italian-style peeled tomatoes, drained and chopped,
    juice reserved
¼ cup chopped fresh basil
Salt and pepper to taste
1 cup Chicken Stock (see page 231)
¼ cup heavy cream
1 pound penne, penne rigate, or tortiglioni
½ cup freshly grated Parmesan cheese

This dish is as colorful as my aunt Ciccina, who made it for us whenever we visited.

Bring a large pot of water, with the 1 tablespoon salt added if desired, to a boil over high heat.

In a large nonstick sauté pan, heat the olive oil over medium-high heat. Add the onion, garlic, sun-dried tomatoes, pine nuts, and chicken, and sauté until the garlic starts to brown, about 4 minutes. Add the brandy

and stir well, and cook for 2 minutes. Add the tomatoes and basil, and cook 2 minutes, stirring well. Salt and pepper to taste, depending on the saltiness of the tomatoes. Add the stock, reserved tomato juice, and cream. Bring to a boil, then simmer for 15 to 20 minutes.

Ten minutes before the sauce is ready, cook the pasta in the boiling water according to the directions on the package. Drain and return to the pot. Pour the sauce over the pasta, and continue to cook over medium-low heat, stirring constantly until the pasta is coated, for 3 to 4 minutes. Remove from heat, add the cheese, stir well, and serve.

Chef's Tip

For an extra dimension in flavor, marinate the chicken breast in a mixture of 2 tablespoons balsamic vinegar, 3 tablespoons olive oil, 1 clove chopped garlic, and 1 tablespoon chopped fresh rosemary overnight. The next day pat the chicken dry and broil until cooked through. Let it cool and then dice. Proceed with the recipe as above.

Pasta with Swordfish, Lemon, and Capers

PASTA CON PESCESPADA E CAPPERI

SERVES 6 GENEROUSLY

1 tablespoon salt (optional)

1½ pounds swordfish steaks

2 tablespoons flour

¾ teaspoon salt

½ teaspoon freshly ground black pepper

6 tablespoons olive oil

6 cloves garlic, thickly sliced

1 cup chopped onion

3 tablespoons drained capers

2 tablespoons chopped fresh Italian parsley, plus 2 tablespoons
   for garnish (optional)

¼ teaspoon red pepper flakes

2 teaspoons grated lemon zest

½ cup white wine

2 cups clam juice

½ cup Tomato Sauce (see page 235)

¼ teaspoon sugar

¼ cup freshly squeezed lemon juice

1 pound lingue di passero, linguine, spaghetti, or spaghettini

You can do much more with swordfish than simple grilling or broiling, and this is just one of the many innovative ways Sicilian chefs have invented to prepare this favorite fish.

Bring a large pot of water, with the 1 tablespoon salt added if desired, to a boil over high heat.

Trim and discard the skin and any very dark red meat from the swordfish. Cut into ½-inch dice. Toss with the flour, ½ teaspoon of the salt, and ¼ teaspoon of the pepper.

In a large sauté pan, heat 3 tablespoons of the olive oil over medium-high heat until sizzling. Cook half of the coated swordfish until golden brown on all sides, about 2 minutes. Remove with a slotted spoon and set aside. Repeat with the remaining fish.

Reduce heat to medium-low, and add the remaining olive oil to the pan. Add the garlic, onion, capers, 2 tablespoons parsley, red pepper flakes, and lemon zest, and cook slowly until the onion is golden and tender, about 5 to 6 minutes. Pour in the white wine and stir gently to dislodge any browned bits from the bottom of the pan. Continue to cook until liquid is reduced by half. Add the clam juice, Tomato Sauce, the remaining salt and pepper, and sugar. Bring to a boil, then simmer for 8 to 10 minutes, until slightly thickened. Add the swordfish, any accumulated juices, and the lemon juice to the sauce, and warm through for 2 minutes.

While the sauce is simmering, cook the pasta in the boiling water according to the directions on the package. Drain and return to the pot. Pour the sauce on the pasta, and simmer over low heat, stirring constantly until the pasta is well coated, for about 2 minutes. Turn the pasta out onto a warm serving dish, sprinkle with 2 tablespoons parsley if desired, and serve.

Nanci

One evening in 1992, my wife, Nanci, and I were celebrating a job offer I'd had from a well-known local restaurant. Over a candlelit dinner with a fine bottle of Brunello di Montalcino at our kitchen table, we reminisced about how I had started in the restaurant business—washing dishes in a trattoria.

It had been something of a struggle giving up my job as a stockbroker to pursue the dream of being a chef. But now, with this new opportunity, the sacrifice and hard work would pay off—or so it seemed. As the evening progressed, the wine worked its magic and we were both relaxed.

Suddenly Nanci burst out laughing, leaned back in her chair, and declared, "Wouldn't it be great to have your own cooking show! Maybe even a book or two. Those guys on TV have nothing on you.

Really, Nick," she continued in response to my look of consternation. "Can you imagine what our life would be like? Now *that's* something to dream about."

Maybe it was the wine talking, but I couldn't help getting caught up in her enthusiasm. Since my training as a stockbroker had turned me into a compulsive note-taker, I grabbed the yellow legal pad that was never far from my side and started jotting down some ideas.

Like many other couples before us, we had a dream, and would try to make it come true. And so, with Louis Armstrong singing "It's a Wonderful World" on the stereo, we sipped our wine and filled many pages with schemes and dreams. Our lives felt full of promise.

The next morning, our cat, Felix (a.k.a. Filippo), woke me up, as usual, at the crack of dawn. Still groggy, I made my way to the kitchen with Felix prancing around my legs. As I was getting his food from the cupboard, I noticed the legal pad we'd abandoned the night before. I fed the cat, then picked up the pad. Through all the scribbles and crossing-out, I was able to decipher some of the ideas we had come up with.

This isn't bad," I said to myself. "Not bad at all." The more I read, the more excited I became. "I can do this!" I said aloud. Felix ignored me.

I had been trained in the art of making cold calls. That's how everyone starts in the stock-trading business. After seven years of practice, I wasn't afraid to ask strangers to invest their money with me. It was the same thing, only this time we would be raising the money to finance a cooking show. That was it for me. I was committed heart and soul. I might be getting in over my head, or maybe I was being carried away by my own enthusiasm, but it felt right. This was the moment to seize the opportunity.

I went back to the bedroom and jumped on the bed, waking Nanci from her deep sleep. "I'm not going to take the new job," I declared. "Let's use the money in our savings to look for investors for the cooking show! It'll be like seed money to start our own production company."

She stared up at me in silence. At that hour of the morning, and with me yammering in her face, I don't know what I was expecting Nanci to say. It wasn't the first time I'd pursued some harebrained notion; I had even given up my job as a stockbroker to work as a dishwasher.

With barely a pause for breath, I went on. "One year," I said, perhaps a bit too defensively in anticipation of her objections. "If it doesn't happen in one year, I'll go back to the restaurant. Come on. What do you say? Let's go for it!" Even though she had come up with the original idea, it took me most of the morning–a few cups of coffee and lots of cajoling–to convince her, but finally she agreed.

One evening two years later, we were again sitting in the kitchen where it all had started. The yellow legal pad was now filled with a sorry version of a budget. We were in trouble. The money was running out. Nanci knew it, and so did I. My faith in our venture had been shaken by too many roadblocks and rejections. At the risk of sounding melodramatic, I have to say there was a sense of impending doom. That evening we tried to avoid the inevitable decision to abandon our dream. We watched an old movie on television, sitting next to each other, holding hands. After Nanci went to bed, I sat in the dark living room, alone with my thoughts and my doubts. It was two in the morning before I roused myself and headed to bed.

I had a long and restless night, and by the first light of dawn I had worked myself into a panic. I stumbled out of bed, taking big breaths to try to calm down. I fell into a big chair on the other side of the room and for a moment thought I might actually stop breathing.

Yet when I looked back toward the bed, I was captivated by a scene that even now I remember with pleasure. The early-morning sunlight was cutting through the blinds into the otherwise dark bedroom. Nanci was sleeping, her breathing soft and steady, a smile playing across her face. Felix was curled up next to her. They looked so vulnerable and carefree that this sight alone quieted my feelings of anxiety. This vision was better than any dream of fame I could have wished for. "Nothing else matters," I thought. "As long as I have her, we are unbeatable!"

I got out of the chair, put on my robe, and walked to the kitchen. With the vision of Nanci sleeping peacefully in the other room, I did what everyone in my family does in times of stress or celebration—I started to cook. Today Nanci's favorite pasta for lunch would be my expression of gratitude for her love and her faith in me.

Later, at the table in our garden, we enjoyed a feast of pasta and wine. Nanci observed I had a strange grin on my face; she wondered what I was thinking.

I remembered something my father told me before I came to America," I said. "Money comes and money goes, but a family—your family—that is forever!"

And on that day, in our little garden, the most important person in my universe was sitting with me. Her eyes sparkled and she laughed aloud. She held my hand, and nothing else mattered.

Entrees

Baked Tuna with Tomato Pesto

Boiled Beef Piedmontese Style

Braised Sea Bass with Peppers and Olives

Chicken Scaloppine with Mushroom Sauce

Chicken Scaloppine with Roasted

Red Pepper Sauce

Chicken Cutlets Milanese Style

Chicken Scaloppine with Sun-Dried Tomatoes and Peas

Lamb Stew with Tomatoes, Garlic, and Rosemary

Braciole

Roasted Chicken with Balsamic Vinegar and Herbs

Roasted Pork Loin with Fennel, Peas, and

Parmesan Sauce

Salmon Scaloppine with Vodka and Caper Sauce

Sausages and Peppers Country Style

Shrimp with Spicy Tomato Sauce

Broiled Marinated Shrimp

Sicilian Barbecue

Sole Fillets with Capers and Lemon Sauce

Stuffed Cabbage Leaves Country Style

Stuffed Turkey Breast

Swordfish Scaloppine "Pizza Style"

Veal Stew with Artichokes and Lemon

Veal Tonnato

Baked Tuna with Tomato Pesto

TONNO ARROSTO CON PESTO DI POMODORO

6 cloves garlic, chopped

½ teaspoon salt

½ teaspoon freshly ground black pepper

¼ teaspoon red pepper flakes

2 tablespoons chopped fresh Italian parsley

2 tablespoons chopped fresh basil

½ cup toasted pine nuts (see tip below)

1 28-ounce can Italian-style peeled tomatoes, drained and chopped

½ teaspoon sugar (optional)

4 tablespoons olive oil, plus extra if baking

6 tuna steaks, about 5 ounces each, 1 inch thick

This type of pesto (the word is translated literally as "paste") is commonly known in Sicily as pesto trapanese, *and originated in the city of Trapani, not far from my father's hometown of Alcamo.*

Preheat the oven, to 425° if baking or to Broil if broiling. (See below.)

Place the garlic, salt, pepper, and red pepper flakes in a large mortar and pound with a pestle into a paste. (If you do not have a large mortar and pestle, use a food processor.) Add the parsley, basil, and pine nuts and grind until smooth. Add the tomatoes and carefully mash to a coarse paste. Add the sugar if the tomatoes are tart. Transfer the paste to a large bowl and whisk in the olive oil.

Smother the tuna steaks with the pesto and marinate in the refrigerator for at least 30 minutes.

To bake: With the oven preheated to 425°, place the marinated tuna steaks with the marinade in a baking pan. Drizzle with olive oil. Bake, uncovered, for 15 minutes, or until the steaks are medium—still nice and pink inside—when checked with a sharp knife.

To broil: Adjust the top rack so it is 3 to 4 inches from the broiler element. With the broiler preheated, place the tuna steaks on a rack or broiler pan and broil for 4 to 5 minutes. Flip over and broil another 2 to 3 minutes, or until the steaks are medium—pink in the center.

Serve immediately with the pesto on the side.

Chef's Tip

The easiest and safest way to toast pine nuts is to toss them with 1 tablespoon olive oil and bake them, on a nonstick baking sheet, in a preheated 325° oven for 5 to 6 minutes.

Boiled Beef Piedmontese Style

MANZO BOLLITO ALLA PIEMONTESE

SERVES 6

2 sprigs fresh thyme, or ¼ teaspoon dried

4 sprigs fresh parsley, plus a cluster for garnish

1 large bay leaf

10 peppercorns, bruised or cracked

3½ pounds first-cut beef brisket or bottom round rump roast, in one piece

7 to 8 cups Beef Stock (see page 233) or 4 14.5-ounce cans

5 or 6 medium carrots, peeled and with ends trimmed, cut into 2-inch pieces

2 pounds potatoes, peeled and cut into 2-to-3-inch chunks

2 cups fresh or frozen peas

Salt and pepper to taste

Twist of lemon peel

1 recipe Green Sauce (see page 247)

In this Italian version of the meal-in-a-pot, the beef becomes fork-tender through the cooking process, which is ideal for cooking tougher cuts of meat. The accompanying green sauce gives a special touch. Note that you'll need kitchen twine for this recipe.

Make a bouquet garni by placing the thyme, 4 sprigs parsley, bay leaf, and peppercorns in a cheesecloth bag, or putting in a square of cheesecloth, gathering the corners together, and tying securely at the top with kitchen twine.

Place the meat and stock in a Dutch oven or a pot wide and deep enough to hold them. The meat should be completely covered by liquid; if necessary, add water. Add the bouquet garni and bring to a boil. When the liquid comes to a boil, skim off the scum. Reduce heat, and cover and simmer until the meat is fork-tender, about 3 hours. It will not hurt to go a bit longer, but undercooking will result in tough meat.

Thirty minutes before the meat has finished cooking, add the carrots and potatoes to the pot. Cover and continue simmering.

While the meat is simmering, make the Green Sauce.

Two minutes before the meat and vegetables are finished cooking, add the frozen peas. Check the meat and vegetables for doneness by carefully piercing with a fork.

When the meat and vegetables are done, remove the meat to a carving board, and remove the vegetables with a slotted spoon and keep warm; discard the bouquet garni. Bring the liquid remaining in the pot to a boil and then reduce for 2 to 3 minutes. Taste for salt and pepper, and season as necessary; if you are using salted canned broth, you won't need to add salt.

Slice the meat into ¼-inch pieces; if there is a layer of fat on the top or bottom, trim before slicing. Line up the slices in the center of a serving dish, slightly overlapping one another. Surround the meat with the cooked mixed vegetables. Ladle some of the cooking liquid over the beef and vegetables, and garnish with parsley sprigs and lemon peel. Serve with the Green Sauce in a separate bowl on the side.

Chef's Tip

You could easily make another sauce to serve along with the green sauce: Boil and reduce the skimmed braising stock by half, and add salt and pepper to taste. Make a paste with 1½ tablespoons softened butter and 1¼ tablespoons flour, and add to the boiling stock, whisking well until the mixture thickens to a saucelike consistency.

Braised Sea Bass with Peppers and Olives

BRANZINO DI PANTELLERIA IN UMIDO

5 tablespoons olive oil

6 Chilean sea bass fillets, about 6 ounces each

⅛ plus ½ teaspoon salt

⅛ plus ¼ tablespoon freshly ground black pepper

1 cup chopped onion

6 cloves garlic, thickly sliced

1 cup diced red bell pepper, cut into ½-inch dice

1 cup diced yellow bell pepper, cut into ½-inch dice

20 black olives, pitted and halved

20 green olives, pitted and halved

2 tablespoons drained capers

3 tablespoons chopped fresh Italian parsley

1 tablespoon chopped fresh basil

¼ teaspoon red pepper flakes

½ cup white wine

½ cup Tomato Sauce (see page 235)

1½ cups clam juice

2 tablespoons freshly squeezed lemon juice

2 tablespoons extra-virgin olive oil

Here is a masterly way of braising a meaty fish like sea bass and making it sing, with an accompanying chorus of melodic flavors.

In a large covered skillet, heat 2 tablespoons of the olive oil over medium-high heat until almost smoking. Pat the fish fillets dry and season with ⅛ teaspoon each of the salt and pepper. Sear the fish in the oil, without jostling, for 3 to 4 minutes, or until a nice brown crust forms. Flip and brown the other side for about 3 minutes. Remove to a plate and cover to keep warm.

Reduce heat to medium. Add the remaining 3 tablespoons olive oil to the skillet, and sauté the onion, garlic, bell peppers, olives, capers, 2 tablespoons of the parsley, basil, red pepper flakes, and remaining ½ teaspoon salt and ¼ teaspoon pepper. Cook, stirring frequently, for 4 to 5 minutes, or until the vegetables soften. Pour in the wine, stirring well to dislodge any browned bits from the bottom of the pan, and continue cooking to reduce liquid by half, 2 to 3 minutes. Add the Tomato Sauce, clam juice, and lemon juice. Bring to a boil, then simmer for 10 to 12 minutes to thicken slightly and strengthen the flavors.

Return the fish fillets to the skillet with the sauce (see tip below). Cover and braise gently over low heat until the fish is tender and opaque throughout, about 8 minutes. Drizzle with the extra-virgin olive oil and garnish with the remaining 1 tablespoon parsley before serving.

Chef's Tip

If your skillet is not big enough to hold the sauce and all the fish fillets, pour the sauce in a large baking pan, place the fillets on top, and bake for 6 to 8 minutes in a preheated 325° oven.

Chicken Scaloppine with Mushroom Sauce

SCALOPPINE DI POLLO CON SALSA DI FUNGHI

SERVES 6

6 boneless, skinless chicken half breasts
½ teaspoon salt
½ teaspoon freshly ground black pepper
¾ cup flour
½ cup olive oil
1 recipe Mushroom Sauce (see page 248)
2 tablespoons chopped fresh parsley (optional)

You will not recognize the chicken here, veiled as it is by a gloriously robust sauce. A quick and simple recipe, yet very elegant.

To prepare the chicken, remove the tenderloin from each half breast; you may freeze for later use. Cut the half breasts across the grain (widthwise) into three slices. Hold your knife at a 20-to-30-degree angle to the cutting board so that you slice on the bias and end up with oval scaloppine. You should get three scaloppine from each half breast. Pound them lightly between pieces of waxed paper or plastic wrap to a thickness of ¼ inch.

Sprinkle with salt and pepper. Dust lightly with the flour, and shake off any excess. In a large saucepan, heat ¼ cup of the olive oil over high heat and quickly brown the half chicken on both sides for 2 to 3 minutes per side. (See tip below.) Remove from heat to a platter, and cover with foil to keep warm. Add the remaining ¼ cup of oil as needed, and repeat the process with the remaining pieces of chicken.

Discard the oil left in the pan. Add the Mushroom Sauce and bring to a boil over high heat, cooking for about 3 to 5 minutes. Add the scaloppine, reduce heat to medium, and cook for 5 minutes.

Place the scaloppine on a serving tray, top with the sauce, and the parsley if desired, and serve. Bring along any extra sauce in a gravy boat.

Chef's Tip

This recipe can be prepared a day ahead, but with the chicken slightly undercooked. To finish it the next day, bring the sauce to a boil, then simmer in the sauce until just heated through.

To drain chicken after browning, use brown paper like that of supermarket bags. It's stronger and more absorbent than paper towels.

Chicken Scaloppine with Roasted Red Pepper Sauce

SCALOPPINE DI POLLO AL SUGO DI PEPERONI ARROSTITI

SERVES 6

6 boneless, skinless chicken half breasts
¼ teaspoon salt
¼ teaspoon freshly ground black pepper
⅓ cup flour
6 tablespoons olive oil
1 cup chopped white onion
6 cloves garlic, thickly sliced
1½ cups finely chopped roasted peeled red bell pepper
½ cup finely chopped honey-glazed ham
½ cup white wine
½ cup Tomato Sauce (see page 235)
1 cup Chicken Stock (see page 231)
3 tablespoons balsamic vinegar
2 tablespoons sugar
¼ cup chopped fresh Italian parsley

Chicken is a perfect match for roasted peppers, which here create an unusual base for the sauce. The dish is finished with just a touch of sweet-and-sour, which lingers on as a gentle good-bye.

To prepare the chicken, remove the tenderloin from each half breast; you may freeze for later use. Cut the half breasts across the grain (widthwise) into three slices. Hold your knife at a 20-to-30-degree angle to the cutting board so that you slice on the bias and end up with oval scaloppine. You should get three scaloppine from each half breast. Pound them lightly between pieces of waxed paper or plastic wrap to a thickness of ¼ inch.

Sprinkle with the salt and pepper. Dust lightly with the flour and shake off any excess. In a large saucepan, heat the olive oil over high heat, and quickly brown the chicken on both sides, 2 to 3 minutes per side. Remove from heat to a platter, and cover with foil to keep warm.

Add the onion, garlic, red bell pepper, and ham to the oil in the pan. Sauté over medium-high heat until the onion is translucent and the garlic starts to brown, 4 to 6 minutes. Add the wine and sauté 2 to 3 minutes. Deglaze the pan, scraping it gently to dislodge any browned bits from the bottom. Add the Tomato Sauce and stock, bring to a boil, then simmer until the liquid is reduced by about a third.

While the sauce is cooking, mix the balsamic vinegar and sugar in a small saucepan and cook on medium heat until the mixture is reduced by half and reaches a thick, syrupy consistency. Add to the sauce just before it is finished.

Return the chicken to the pan, sprinkle with the parsley, and sauté another 3 to 5 minutes, until the chicken is cooked through. Serve.

Chef's Tip

If your skillet is not big enough to hold the sauce and all the chicken, pour the sauce into a large baking pan, place the chicken on top, and bake for 6 to 8 minutes in a preheated 325° oven.

While roasted red peppers from a jar or can are perfectly acceptable in cooking, the flavor of a freshly roasted pepper is far superior. If you use jarred or canned peppers, rinse them in cool water and soak them in additional cool water for a few minutes to remove the tannic flavor.

To roast your own peppers, place the whole peppers in your pre-heated broiler, 3 to 4 inches from the heat source. Turn the peppers with tongs as they start to brown and blister. Don't allow them to turn black, as that will produce a bitter taste. When they are roasted on all sides, remove them and place them in a paper bag. Seal the bag and allow the peppers to cool. One they are cooled, the skin will fall away easily. Carefully remove the skins, stems, and seeds, and use the peppers according to your recipe.

Peppers can also be roasted over the flame of a gas stove. This is a little trickier, as they can burn quite easily. Hold the pepper over the flame with tongs until all sides are brown and blistered. Remove to a paper bag, and follow further directions above.

Chicken Cutlets Milanese Style

COTOLETTE DI POLLO ALLA MILANESE

SERVES 6

As the name implies, this dish comes from Milan, where more common versions are made with beef or veal. My mother used to refer to it as "popcorn chicken" because my brother Mario, who was in love with this American snack food, would eat anything with that name.

6 boneless, skinless chicken half breasts

¼ teaspoon salt

¼ teaspoon freshly ground black pepper, plus additional to taste

1 cup plus 2 tablespoons flour

3 eggs, lightly beaten

2 cups Italian-Style Bread Crumbs (see page 230)

¾ cup olive oil

6 cloves garlic, thickly sliced

1 cup diced white onion

4 ounces prosciutto or ham, finely chopped

½ cup white wine

1½ cups Chicken Stock (see page 231)

½ cup heavy cream

2 tablespoons chopped lemon zest

1½ tablespoons freshly squeezed lemon juice

1 tablespoon chopped fresh Italian parsley

To prepare the chicken, remove the tenderloin from each half breast; you may freeze for later use. Cut the half breasts across the grain (widthwise) into three slices. Hold your knife at a 20-to-30-degree angle to the cutting board so that you slice on the bias and end up with oval scaloppine. You should get three from each half breast. Pound them lightly between pieces of waxed paper or plastic wrap to a thickness of ¼ inch. Sprinkle them with the salt and pepper. Dust lightly with the 1 cup flour, and shake off any excess.

Put the beaten eggs and bread crumbs in separate deep dishes or pie tins. Dip each piece of chicken in the eggs, then hold it over the dish to allow any excess egg to drip back in the dish. Then place the chicken in the bread crumbs and press down firmly. Gently turn over, and press the other side down firmly into the crumbs. Remove the chicken from the bread crumbs, lightly shaking off any loose crumbs, and place on a sheet pan. Once breaded, your scaloppine are *cotolette,* or cutlets.

Preheat oven to 200°.

In a large (at least 12-inch) sauté pan, heat ½ cup of the olive oil over medium-high heat. Fry the cutlets in the oil, gently turning until golden brown on both sides, 2 to 3 minutes per side. You may have to do this in batches to avoid burning the chicken. Drain the fried cutlets on brown paper to draw off excess oil. Place the cutlets on a sheet pan and cover with foil and keep them in the warm oven. When you have fried all the cutlets, dispose of the cooking oil.

To make the sauce, heat the remaining ¼ cup of the olive oil in the same pan over medium-high heat, and add the garlic, onion, and ham. Sauté until the onion is translucent and the garlic and ham start to brown, 4 to 6 minutes. Add the wine, and deglaze the pan by scraping it gently to dislodge any browned pieces from the bottom of the pan. Remove from heat. Gradually sprinkle the 2 tablespoons of flour into the pan, and stir well to incorporate.

Return to heat, add the stock and the cream, and stir well to incorporate the ingredients. Bring to a boil, and reduce heat to simmer. Allow to cook for 12 to 15 minutes, or until mixture reaches a saucelike consistency; it is the proper consistency when it coats the back of a spoon.

Add the lemon zest and pepper to taste, and simmer for 2 to 3 minutes. Remove from heat and carefully add the lemon juice, stirring constantly to prevent the cream from curdling.

Remove the cutlets from the oven to a large serving platter, top with the sauce, sprinkle with the parsley, and serve.

Pasta with Sausage and Pumpkin Sauce

Braised Sea Bass with
Peppers and Olives (right)

 Pasta with Shrimp and Artichokes

Chicken Scaloppine with Mushroom Sauce, and Grandma's Polenta

Chicken Scaloppine with Sun-Dried Tomatoes and Peas

SCALOPPINE DI POLLO AL SUGO DI POMODORI SECCHI

SERVES 6

6 boneless, skinless chicken half breasts

¼ teaspoon salt

¼ teaspoon freshly ground black pepper

⅓ cup flour

6 tablespoons olive oil

1 cup chopped white onion

6 cloves garlic, thickly sliced

1¼ cups coarsely chopped sun-dried tomatoes packed in olive oil,
     drained before chopping

½ cup full-bodied red wine

1 cup Tomato Sauce (see page 235)

1 cup Chicken Stock (see page 231)

1½ cups fresh or frozen peas

Salt and pepper to taste

2 tablespoons chopped fresh Italian parsley

This chicken dish features a rustic flavor, spiked by the sun-dried tomatoes and sweetened by the green peas. It looks great, and it tastes even better!

To prepare the chicken, remove the tenderloin from each half breast; you may freeze for later use. Cut the half breasts across the grain (widthwise) into three slices. Hold your knife at a 20-to-30-degree angle to the cutting board so that you slice on the bias and end up with oval scaloppine. You should get three scaloppine from each half breast. Pound them lightly between pieces of waxed paper or plastic wrap to a thickness of ¼ inch.

Sprinkle with ¼ teaspoon each salt and pepper. Dust lightly with the flour, and shake off any excess. In a large saucepan, heat the olive oil over high heat, and quickly brown the chicken on both sides, 2 to 3 minutes per side. You will have to do this in batches. Remove from heat to a platter, and cover with foil to keep warm.

Add the onion, garlic, and sun-dried tomatoes to the oil in the pan. Sauté over medium-high heat until the onion is translucent and the garlic starts to brown, about 4 to 6 minutes. Add the wine, and sauté for 2 to 3 minutes, deglazing the pan to dislodge any browned bits from the bottom. Add the Tomato Sauce and stock, and bring to a boil. Add the peas, and simmer until the sauce is reduced by half, about 10 to 12 minutes. Add salt and pepper to taste.

Return the chicken to the sauce until heated through, 2 to 3 minutes (see tip below), sprinkle with the parsley, and serve.

Chef's Tip

If the pan is not big enough to hold all the chicken and the sauce, pour the sauce into a large baking pan, place the scaloppine on top, and re-heat in a preheated 350° oven for 3 to 5 minutes.

Lamb Stew with Tomatoes, Garlic, and Rosemary

SPEZZATINO DI AGNELLO AL SUGO DI POMODORO

SERVES 6

½ cup flour

1 teaspoon salt

½ teaspoon freshly ground black pepper

3 to 3¼ pounds lamb stew meat (boneless leg), cut into 1½-to-2-inch pieces

6 tablespoons olive oil

6 large cloves garlic, thickly sliced

½ large white onion, cut in half lengthwise and sliced thinly horizontally

1 heaping tablespoon finely chopped fresh rosemary

¼ teaspoon red pepper flakes

2 14.5-ounce cans Italian-style stewed tomatoes, drained and chopped into large pieces, juice reserved

1 tablespoon plus ¼ cup chopped fresh mint

1 cup red wine

3 cups Beef Stock (see page 233)

2 15-ounce cans cannellini (or Great Northern or navy beans), drained and rinsed

Salt and pepper to taste

¼ cup chopped fresh parsley

Sicilian farmers revere this dish as a gift from the gods. My father asked for it whenever we went to visit my grandma Maria in Alcamo. The first thing she would say, welcoming him with a hug at the door, was: "I made stew for my favorite picciriddu [little boy]." When it comes to food, we all remain children in the eyes of our parents.

Combine the flour, salt, and pepper in a large plate or bowl. Toss in the lamb, a few pieces at a time, to coat lightly.

In a Dutch oven, heat 3 tablespoons of the olive oil over medium-high heat. Brush any excess flour off the lamb, and brown in the oil. You will have to do this in batches. Remove each browned batch, set aside, and cover to keep warm. Add a tablespoon of oil and heat well before each new batch, as necessary.

In the same pot, heat 1 tablespoon olive oil over medium-high heat. Add the garlic, onion, rosemary, and red pepper flakes, and cook until the garlic starts to brown, stirring well to dislodge any browned bits from the bottom of the pot, about 3 minutes. Add the tomatoes and cook until dry, 3 to 4 minutes. Add the 1 tablespoon mint and return the lamb to the pot. Toss well to coat.

Deglaze the pot with the wine, gently scraping to dislodge any browned bits from the bottom. Bring to a boil, and continue cooking to reduce liquid by half.

Add the reserved tomato juice (about 1½ cups) and stock. Bring to a boil, then simmer, partially covered, for 1 hour. Stir occasionally. Uncover and cook for 15 minutes more. Add the beans. Cook, uncovered, for 5 to 10 minutes, until sauce is desired thickness and meat is tender.

Add salt and pepper to taste. Stir in the ¼ cup mint and parsley, and serve.

Braciole

SERVES 6

1 recipe Mashed Potatoes Parmesan (see page 76)

2 tablespoons softened butter (optional)

1½ tablespoons flour (optional)

2 to 2¼ pounds beef prepared for scaloppine (18 3-by-3-inch pieces, pounded
  ⅛ to ¼ inch thick; see tip below)

¾ pound Asiago cheese, thinly sliced into 18 equal portions (see tip below)

18 large whole basil leaves

6 ounces prosciutto or ham, chopped and divided into 18 equal portions

¼ cup flour

¼ teaspoon salt

½ teaspoon freshly ground black pepper

5 tablespoons olive oil

Pinch red pepper flakes

4 cloves garlic, thickly sliced

½ cup finely diced white onion

1½ cups white wine

1½ cups Chicken Stock (see page 231)

¼ cup plus 2 tablespoons chopped parsley

When you say "braciole" to a meat-eating Italian, watch the body language as the word is heard. The eyes roll back, while the hands, instinctively close in an imaginary pinch, move up and down. In some cases the tongue darts out, as if licking the chops still moist with sauce. But don't laugh—try this recipe, and next time you hear the word, see what happens to you.

Prepare the potatoes and keep warm.

Make a paste of the softened butter and the 1½ tablespoons flour, and set aside. (You may use this to thicken the sauce later.)

To prepare the braciole: Place the beef slices separately on a flat surface. Top each with 1 portion cheese, 1 basil leaf, and 1 portion prosciutto. Fold in half, making a pocket, and secure the ends with a long toothpick. Tuck in any prosciutto or cheese that extends outside the pocket. Keep one end of the toothpicks visible for easy removal after cooking.

In a shallow bowl or rimmed plate, mix the ¼ cup flour, salt, and pepper. Gently dip each meat pocket into the flour mixture and coat thoroughly. Shake off any excess flour.

In a large sauté pan, heat 2 tablespoons of the olive oil over high heat. When the oil is hot, put 6 meat pockets in the pan. Cook until well browned, at least 1 to 2 minutes per side. Remove the browned meat to a plate. Repeat with the remaining meat pockets, adding more oil as needed before browning, and letting it heat well before adding the meat.

After removing all the browned meat, heat 1 tablespoon oil in the pan. Add the red pepper flakes and garlic, and sauté over medium heat until garlic is light brown, about 3 minutes. Add the onion and sauté until soft, about 3 to 4 minutes.

Preheat oven to 200°.

Deglaze the pan with the wine. Bring to a boil, and continue cooking to reduce liquid by half. Add the stock, bring to a boil, and then simmer until sauce starts to thicken slightly, about 10 to 12 minutes. Stir in the ¼ cup parsley.

Add the meat pockets to the sauce in the pan, and spoon the sauce over the top to coat completely. Cook until heated through, 2 to 3 minutes. (You may have to do this in two batches if your pan is not large enough.)

Remove the meat to a serving tray and place in the oven.

If the sauce is not thick enough for you, bring back to a boil and add the butter-flour paste, half at a time, and cook for 2 to 3 minutes.

Remove the meat from the oven, and the toothpicks from the meat. To serve elegantly, fan 3 braciole on each dinner plate next to the potatoes. Pour the sauce around the braciole and sprinkle with the 2 tablespoons parsley.

Chef's Tip

You may use a semisoft, sliceable mild cheese instead of the Asiago. Fontina is a nice, stronger-tasting alternative.

Roasted Chicken with Balsamic Vinegar and Herbs

POLLO ARROSTO CON ACETO BALSAMICO

SERVES 6

Marinated in a magical concoction of oil, vinegar, and fresh herbs, everyday chicken is transformed. This dish is as simple to make as it is impressive to serve, so you'll be able to enjoy your own dinner party, as well as the compliments. You'll need to start a day in advance, to allow for the marinating time.

DAY 1
2 2½-pound chickens, cut into standard quarters (legs and breasts)

2 teaspoons salt

2 teaspoons freshly ground black pepper

2 cups chopped yellow onion

3 tablespoons chopped garlic

2 tablespoons chopped fresh rosemary

2 tablespoons chopped fresh sage

3 tablespoons chopped fresh parsley

3 tablespoons chopped fresh basil

¾ cup olive oil

¾ cup balsamic vinegar

DAY 2
2 pounds red rose potatoes, peeled and cut into 1-inch cubes

½ teaspoon salt

⅛ teaspoon pepper

2 tablespoons olive oil

2 14.5-ounce cans chicken stock

2 tablespoons cornstarch

¼ cup cold water

The day before you intend to serve the dish, rinse and trim the chicken and cut into pieces. Salt and pepper on both sides. Lay the pieces flat, skin side up, in a glass baking dish, and sprinkle with the onion, garlic, and herbs. Mix the oil and vinegar, pour over the chicken, then cover with plastic wrap and refrigerate. Turn the pieces once or twice while in the marinade.

The day of serving, preheat oven to 375°.

Sprinkle the potatoes with the salt and pepper, and coat with the olive oil. Set aside.

Remove the chicken from the marinade. Strain the marinade through a fine sieve, and reserve for making the gravy.

Place the potatoes in a large roasting pan, and the chicken pieces, skin side down, on top. Bake for 30 minutes. Turn the chicken over, skin side up, and bake for 45 minutes, or until the chicken is golden brown with a crispy skin. Remove to a platter and cover with foil to keep warm.

Increase oven temperature to 450°, and roast the potatoes for 15 to 20 minutes, or until they are soft in the center when tested with a fork. Remove to the platter with the chicken, and cover with foil to keep warm.

Put the roasting pan on a stovetop burner over medium-high heat. (If the pan cannot be placed on a burner, transfer the contents to a sauté pan or saucepan.) Deglaze the pan with the strained marinade, scraping gently to dislodge any browned bits from the bottom. Add the stock and bring to a boil, then cook for 5 minutes.

Mix the cornstarch with the cold water until smooth and add to the sauce in the pan, stirring well (see tip below). Boil for 2 to 3 minutes, or until thickened. Ladle some of the sauce over the chicken and potatoes, and place the remainder in a gravy boat. The masterpiece is ready to serve.

Chef's Tip

An alternative to the cornstarch paste can be made from 2 tablespoons softened butter and 1½ tablespoons flour. Add this to the boiling sauce to thicken it.

Roasted Pork Loin with Fennel, Peas, and Parmesan Sauce

MAIALE ARROSTO CON FINOCCHIO AL SUGO PARMIGIANO

SERVES 6

3 pounds boneless pork loin, in one piece

1½ teaspoons salt

1 teaspoon freshly ground black pepper

3½ tablespoons olive oil

1 cup finely diced celery (3 medium stalks)

1 cup finely diced carrot (2 medium)

1 cup finely diced white onion (½ large)

4 to 5 ounces pancetta or bacon, finely diced

1 cup white wine

1 to 1½ pounds fennel, bulbs only (stalks and feathery ends removed),
   cleaned, cored, and cut into eighths

10 whole cloves garlic, peeled

1½ cups Chicken Stock (see page 231)

1 cup heavy cream

¾ cup frozen peas, thawed

1 cup freshly grated Parmesan cheese

One thing I've learned from my father is that sometimes you just have to put business on hold, invite some friends over for dinner, and make some great food and drink some fine wine. These recipes may take time, but it is worth every minute.

Preheat oven to 325°.

Season the pork on all sides with the salt and pepper.

In a large, deep sauté pan, heat the oil over medium-high heat. When the oil is hot, brown the roast on all sides, at least a few minutes per side so it gets nice and brown. Remove to a plate and set aside.

In the same pan, sauté the celery, carrot, onion, and pancetta over medium heat for about 8 to 10 minutes. Add the wine, stirring well to dislodge any browned bits from the bottom of the pan. Continue cooking to reduce liquid for about 4 to 5 minutes.

Line the bottom of a small roasting pan with the fennel, garlic, stock, and cream. Add the pork and pour over it the mixture from the pan; use a spatula to remove any good little bits of chopped vegetables and pancetta. Roast in the oven for about an hour, turning the meat every 15 to 20 minutes to keep it moist. When the meat is done, it should be slightly pink on the inside (see tip below). Remove the roast and fennel, and set aside. Let the roast sit for at least 15 minutes before slicing.

Put the roasting pan on a stovetop burner over medium heat. (If the pan cannot be placed on a burner, transfer the contents to a sauté pan or saucepan.) Bring the contents to a boil, then simmer, reducing to a saucelike consistency, for 8 to 10 minutes. Add the peas and cook for 2 minutes. Stir in the cheese until melted. Remove from heat.

Slice the pork, no more than ¼ inch thick, and lay overlapping slices on a platter or on individual plates. Spoon the sauce on top, making sure to include bits of chopped vegetable and pancetta. Surround the meat with fennel, peas, and more sauce.

Chef's Tip

Measure the temperature with a meat thermometer, and remove the pork from the oven when the internal temperature is 165° to 170°. The meat will continue to cook as it stands waiting to be carved. It should be slightly pink inside, with a juicy consistency.

Salmon Scaloppine with Vodka and Caper Sauce

SCALOPPINE DI SALMONE AL SUGO DI VODKA E CAPPERI

SERVES 6 TO 8

2¾ to 3 pounds center-cut salmon fillet, skinned
½ teaspoon salt
¼ teaspoon freshly ground black pepper
1¼ cups flour
6 tablespoons olive oil
4 tablespoons finely chopped shallots
2 tablespoons rinsed and drained capers
6 tablespoons chopped fresh dill
6 tablespoons vodka
4 tablespoons clam juice
¾ cup heavy cream
¾ cup Tomato Sauce (see page 235)
4 tablespoons chopped fresh Italian parsley
Salt and pepper to taste
1 recipe Sautéed Spinach (see page 78)

This is by no means a Sicilian recipe, but it became one in our household when my father experimented with a bottle of Russian vodka.

To prepare the salmon scaloppine, cut the fillet at a 20-to-30-degree angle with a very sharp slicing or carving knife. The scaloppine should be about ½ inch thick and 3 inches long. Sprinkle them with the salt and pepper, and dust them in the flour, shaking off any excess. In a large sauté pan, heat 2 to 3 tablespoons of the olive oil over high heat. When the oil is hot, quickly brown the scaloppine, cooking for no more than 1 to 2 minutes. To prevent overcooking, brown in small batches. Remove the browned scaloppine to a plate and set aside.

In the same pan, adding more oil as necessary, sauté the shallots until translucent and brown-edged, about 2 to 3 minutes. Add the capers and dill, then the vodka, scraping gently to dislodge any browned bits from the bottom of the pan. Be careful, as vodka may flame up; if it does, stand back and wait for the flame to die down.

Add the clam juice, cream, and Tomato Sauce. Bring to a boil, then simmer until reduced to a saucelike consistency, 12 to 15 minutes. The sauce has reached the proper consistency when it coats the back of a spoon.

Prepare the Sautéed Spinach.

Return the scaloppine to the pan with the sauce (see tip below), add the parsley, and season with salt and pepper to taste. Let salmon cook for another 1 to 2 minutes, or until cooked through.

Place the Sautéed Spinach on a large platter, arrange the salmon scaloppine around it, and ladle some of the sauce over the salmon. Pour the remaining sauce in a gravy boat, and serve.

Chef's Tip

If the pan isn't large enough to accommodate all the salmon and the sauce, put the scaloppine in a large baking dish, cover with the finished sauce, and reheat for 2 to 3 minutes in a preheated 325° oven.

Sausages and Peppers Country Style

SALSICCE E PEPERONI ALLA CONTADINA

SERVES 6 GENEROUSLY

4 tablespoons olive oil

8 spicy or sweet Italian sausages (1½ to 2 pounds total)

1 red bell pepper, thinly sliced

1 yellow bell pepper, thinly sliced

1 medium onion, sliced

6 cloves garlic, thickly sliced

¼ teaspoon red pepper flakes

4 tablespoons chopped fresh Italian parsley

2 teaspoons chopped fresh rosemary

½ cup white wine

1 14.5-ounce can Italian-style stewed tomatoes, drained and chopped,
   juice reserved

½ teaspoon salt

½ teaspoon freshly ground black pepper

1 recipe Grandma's Polenta (see page 77)

Although the ingredients in this recipe seem to be assembled casually, they respond to a grand design. Yet I think that my grandmother knew the real secret of this dish—the unhurried cooking of the sausage accompanied by a joyful song. Whenever we heard her singing in the kitchen we knew that a feast of sausages was in the making.

In a large sauté pan, heat 2 tablespoons of the olive oil over medium-high heat. When the oil is hot, brown the sausages on all sides. Remove the sausages to a big plate, slice each into thirds for easier serving, and cover to keep warm. In the same pan, in the oil left from the sausages, fry the bell peppers over high heat until just brown, about 3 to 4 minutes. Transfer to the plate with the sausages. Add the remaining 2 tablespoons olive oil to the pan, reduce heat to medium. When the oil is hot, add the onion, garlic, red pepper flakes, 2 tablespoons of the parsley, and rosemary until the onion is tender, about 6 to 8 minutes. Add the wine, stirring gently to dislodge any browned bits from the bottom of the pan. Continue cooking to reduce liquid by half, for about 3 to 4 minutes.

Add the tomatoes, salt, and pepper, and cook until nearly dry, about 7 to 8 minutes. Return the sausages and peppers to the pan, and add the reserved tomato juice, stirring to incorporate. Bring to a boil, then simmer, stirring often, until the sausages are cooked through and the sauce has thickened, about 15 minutes.

While this mixture is simmering, make the polenta. Pour the finished polenta onto a warm serving dish, top with the sausage-and-pepper mixture, sprinkle with the remaining parsley, and serve.

Shrimp with Spicy Tomato Sauce

GAMBERI AL SUGO PICCANTE DI POMODORO

SERVES 6

1½ pounds shrimp, peeled and deveined (21 to 25 per pound)
½ teaspoon salt
½ teaspoon freshly ground black pepper
1 cup flour
1½ teaspoons paprika
6 to 8 tablespoons olive oil
5 cloves garlic, thickly sliced
1 tablespoon red pepper flakes
2 tablespoons chopped fresh Italian parsley
¾ cup white wine
15 ounces clam juice
1 cup Spicy Tomato Sauce (see page 238)
1½ tablespoons freshly squeezed lemon juice

Here's a very easy recipe for an unforgettable dish. The delicate shrimp go wonderfully with the aggressive sauce. As they say, opposites attract.

Rinse the shrimp in cold water and pat dry. Sprinkle with the salt and pepper. In a shallow pan, mix the flour and paprika, and generously dust the shrimp with the mixture.

In a large 12-inch skillet, heat 2 tablespoons of the olive oil over medium-high heat until rippling. In batches of no more than 8 or 9 at a time, cook shrimp for 30 seconds per side; add oil as necessary as you add shrimp to the pan. The flour should form a crusty coating on the shrimp; the shrimp should be slightly brown but undercooked. Remove each batch to a platter and cover with foil.

In the same skillet, heat 2 tablespoons of the oil over medium heat. Add the garlic and red pepper flakes and cook until garlic is brown, 3 to 5 minutes. Add the parsley, then the wine, stirring to dislodge any browned bits from the bottom of the pan. Increase heat to high, and simmer to reduce liquid to a third of the original volume, about 4 to 6 minutes.

Add the clam juice and Spicy Tomato Sauce, and bring to a boil. Reduce heat and simmer until the sauce reaches the proper consistency, thick enough to coat the back of a spoon, about 10 to 12 minutes.

Place the shrimp in the sauce and cook for 2 to 3 minutes. To test for doneness, check the spine of the shrimp: the flesh should be pink and opaque. Pour the lemon juice over the sauce, stir gently, and serve.

Broiled Marinated Shrimp

GAMBERI AL FORNO

SERVES 6 GENEROUSLY

6 cloves garlic, chopped
½ cup freshly squeezed lemon juice
2 tablespoons chopped fresh Italian parsley
1 tablespoon chopped fresh basil
2 teaspoons chopped fresh sage
1 teaspoon chopped fresh rosemary
½ teaspoon red pepper flakes
½ teaspoon salt
½ teaspoon freshly ground black pepper
1 cup olive oil
18 jumbo shrimp, in shells (8 to 10 per pound)
½ cup Italian-Style Bread Crumbs (see page 230)

Prepare the marinade: In a large bowl, mix the garlic, lemon juice, fresh herbs, red pepper flakes, salt, and pepper. Whisk in the olive oil.

Pull the tiny legs off the shrimp, and with a large, sharp knife, slice the shrimp in half lengthwise, leaving the shell on. Put the shrimp in the marinade and leave to absorb the flavors for at least 30 but no more than 45 minutes.

Place an oven rack 3 to 4 inches below the broiler. Preheat to broil.

Remove the shrimp from the marinade and dip the sliced half into the bread crumbs. Place crumb side up on a broiling pan. Broil until just cooked through, with the bread crumbs nicely browned, about 3 to 4 minutes. Serve hot.

This recipe was the by-product of a bad meal at a small trattoria on the northern Sicilian coast near Cefalù. My father was so upset by the poorly cooked shrimp that he vowed to create the ultimate shrimp recipe, and this is what he came up with. You will forever thank that hapless chef in Cefalù.

Alternatively, preheat an outdoor grill to medium-high heat. Grill the breaded shrimp shell side down for 3 minutes, then turn and grill shell side up for 2 minutes, or until the bread crumbs are toasted brown and the shrimp have curled slightly.

Sicilian Barbecue

CARNI MISTE ALLA GRIGLIA

SERVES 6

MARINADE
½ cup chopped yellow or sweet onion
¼ loosely packed cup parsley leaves, washed and dried
Pinch red pepper flakes
8 fresh basil leaves
2 fresh sage leaves
¼ teaspoon dried thyme
¼ teaspoon dried oregano
1 teaspoon fresh rosemary leaves
¼ cup freshly squeezed lemon juice
½ cup white wine
½ cup extra-virgin olive oil
1 bay leaf
15 peppercorns, cracked

MEAT AND VEGETABLES
¾ pound boneless sirloin, cut into 2-inch cubes
¾ pound boneless pork loin, cut into 2-inch cubes
¾ pound butterflied leg of lamb, cut into 2-inch cubes
¾ pound veal shoulder, cut into 2-inch cubes
2 red bell peppers, trimmed and cut into 2-inch squares or diamonds
2 yellow bell peppers, trimmed and cut into 2-inch squares or diamonds
2 medium Spanish or sweet onions, peeled and cut into 1½-inch chunks
Salt and pepper to taste

As a young man I found no greater joy than to assist my father barbecuing. You can find the same joy: make this your special barbecue recipe, and don't let a summer go by without showing off some of your Sicilian cooking. In case summer is too far away, though, I include instructions for indoor cooking. Note that you'll need to prepare the marinade—and marinate—the day before cooking.

Prepare the marinade: Place the onion, parsley, red pepper flakes, fresh and dried herbs, lemon juice, and wine in a blender or food processor. Process until ingredients are well blended. With the motor running, slowly add the olive oil, and process until well emulsified. Pour into a large glass bowl. Add the bay leaf and peppercorns.

Place the cubed meat into the bowl of marinade. Toss well to coat. Cover the bowl with plastic wrap and refrigerate overnight. Stir occasionally to recoat.

The next day, assemble the meat and vegetables on skewers. Use one of each kind of meat per skewer, alternating with the vegetables—for example, red pepper, beef, yellow pepper, veal, onion, lamb, red pepper, pork, yellow pepper. Brush with the marinade, and sprinkle with salt and pepper to taste. Now you're ready to cook, outdoors or in.

To barbecue: Preheat the outdoor gas barbecue grill to medium-high. For coals, set the grill rack about 4 inches over white-hot coals.

Grill the skewered meats and vegetables for a total of 10 minutes, turning every few minutes and brushing with the marinade at every turn. Move the meat toward the cooler part of the grill and let it stand for 2 more minutes, turning once. Check for doneness, and serve when done.

To broil: Place the skewered meat in a broiling pan. After about 5 minutes, when the meat and vegetables begin to brown, turn and broil for about 5 more minutes, until done. The amount of time it takes to cook the meat depends on the distance from the broiler. Check for doneness, and serve when done.

Sole Fillets with Capers and Lemon Sauce

FILLETTI DI SOGLIOLA CON CAPPERI E LIMONE

SERVES 6 GENEROUSLY

1 recipe Saffroned Rice Timbales (see page 79)
¼ cup flour
¾ teaspoon salt
¾ teaspoon freshly ground black pepper
6 large or 12 small sole fillets, skinned and boned (1¾ pounds total)
6 tablespoons olive oil
¼ cup finely chopped shallot
4 cloves garlic, thickly sliced
3 tablespoons chopped fresh Italian parsley
⅛ teaspoon red pepper flakes
¾ cup white wine
1 cup clam juice
¼ cup drained capers
2 tablespoons freshly squeezed lemon juice

The tender flavor of the sole here shines through a delicate sauce. This is ideal for a light, flavorful late-night supper.

Prepare the timbales.

In a shallow dish or plate, combine the flour and ½ teaspoon each of the salt and pepper. Coat the sole fillets in the seasoned flour; tap off any excess flour.

In a large sauté pan, heat 4 tablespoons of the olive oil over medium-high heat. When the oil is hot, add a few sole fillets, and sear until golden brown and just opaque, about 1 to 2 minutes per side. Agitate the fish as little as possible while cooking, to get the best color and shape. When done, remove the fish to a plate. Repeat in batches with the remaining fillets.

Reduce heat to medium-low and swirl the remaining 2 tablespoons olive oil into the pan. Sauté the shallot, garlic, 2 tablespoons of the parsley, and red pepper flakes until the shallot is tender and just brown, about 3 to 4 minutes. Deglaze with the wine, stirring gently to dislodge any browned bits from the bottom of the pan. Continue cooking to reduce liquid by half.

Add the clam juice, capers, and the remaining ¼ teaspoon each salt and pepper. Bring to a boil, then simmer until the sauce is thickened slightly, 10 to 12 minutes. Pour half of the sauce into another sauté pan (see tip below) and cook over medium heat. Stir in 1 tablespoon lemon juice into each of the pans, and carefully place equal numbers of the sole fillets in each to warm through, for about 2 to 3 minutes. Sprinkle evenly with the remaining parsley, and serve immediately with the unmolded timbales.

Chef's Tip

It's unlikely you have a pan large enough to hold all the fish fillets at once without breaking them; that's the reason for dividing the sauce between the two pans. You might also put the fillets in a large baking pan and cover them with the warm sauce, then finish cooking in a preheated 325° oven for 3 minutes.

Stuffed Cabbage Leaves Country Style

FAGOTTINI DI VERZA FARCITI

SERVES 6 GENEROUSLY

2 carrots, peeled or scraped

2 stalks celery, ends trimmed

1 medium onion, peeled

4 tablespoons plus 2 teaspoons olive oil

1 pound spicy Italian sausage, casing removed

1 tablespoon chopped fresh Italian parsley

6 cloves garlic, thickly sliced

¼ teaspoon red pepper flakes

1 cup red wine

1 cup Tomato Sauce (see page 235)

½ cup Chicken Stock (see page 231)

1 cup freshly grated Romano cheese

½ cup Italian-Style Bread Crumbs (see page 230)

½ teaspoon salt

½ teaspoon freshly ground black pepper

6 large cabbage leaves (about 9 inches in diameter), or 12 medium
    (about 7 inches in diameter) (see tip below)

1 recipe Spicy Tomato Sauce (see page 238)

This unusual dish comes from northern Italy. My Venetian grandma Adele often prepared these delicacies for my mother, her brothers and sisters. While the recipe calls for the most common ingredients, the result is of flawless elegance.

Preheat oven to 375°.

Make a *soffritto*, a flavorful vegetable base, by finely chopping together the carrots, celery, and onion in a food processor, about 10 to 12 quick pulses.

In a large sauté pan, heat the 4 tablespoons olive oil over medium heat. Add the *soffritto,* sausage, parsley, garlic, and red pepper flakes. Sauté, breaking the sausage into small pieces, until the onion is tender and the meat is nicely browned, about 10 to 12 minutes. Add the wine, stirring to dislodge any browned bits from the bottom of the pan. Increase heat and continue cooking to reduce liquid by half.

Pour in the Tomato Sauce and stock. Bring to a boil, then simmer 10 to 12 minutes, or until the mixture is thick and rich. Remove from heat and let cool slightly.

Stir the cheese and bread crumbs into the cooled mixture, and season with the salt and pepper. This is the stuffing for the cabbage leaves.

To stuff them, arrange on a flat surface and spoon about ¾ cup of the stuffing into the center of each leaf. Fold the leaf around the stuffing as you would an envelope. Carefully turn the cabbage rolls over so the loose ends face down. Secure the rolls with kitchen twine, tying them like small packages. Place the rolls in a baking pan lightly greased with oil. Drizzle with the 2 teaspoons olive oil and bake for 25 to 30 minutes, or until the cabbage is lightly browned and the juices start to run.

While the cabbage rolls are baking, prepare the Spicy Tomato Sauce. Serve alongside the stuffed cabbage.

Chef's Tip

To remove cabbage leaves from a fresh head without breaking them, try either of these techniques:

Set the head of cabbage in boiling water for 2 to 3 minutes. Remove the cabbage from the water carefully with tongs or a large slotted spoon, and rinse in cold water. Two or three of the large outside leaves should peel off without cracking. Repeat placing the cabbage in the boiling water and removing two or three outer leaves until you have enough for the recipe.

Or remove the core from the bottom of the cabbage and peel off the raw leaves. Parboil the leaves in salted boiling water for 1 to 2 minutes, or until tender, and rinse in cold water.

To remove the hard rib from a cabbage leaf, cut a 1-inch triangle from the tough bottom section.

Stuffed Turkey Breast

PETTO DI TACCHINO FARCITO

SERVES 6

Maybe next Thanksgiving, when you're looking for a novel way to prepare turkey, you will remember this old-fashioned Italian recipe.

OMELET
1 tablespoon unsalted butter
2 large eggs
2 tablespoons water
⅛ teaspoon salt
⅛ teaspoon pepper
1 tablespoon chopped fresh parsley
1 tablespoon chopped fresh basil
1 tablespoon chopped fresh sage
1 teaspoon dried thyme
2 tablespoons freshly grated or shredded Parmesan cheese

MUSHROOM MIXTURE
3 tablespoons olive oil
1 pound cremini white button mushrooms, sliced ¼ inch thick
½ teaspoon red pepper flakes
4 ounces prosciutto or ham, chopped
½ teaspoon coarse salt
¼ teaspoon freshly ground black pepper
5 large cloves garlic, finely chopped
½ cup brandy

TURKEY
2½ to 3 pounds whole boneless turkey breasts (breasts separated)
½ teaspoon salt
¼ teaspoon freshly ground black pepper

¼ cup flour, seasoned with salt and pepper

3 tablespoons olive oil

½ cup brandy

1 cup heavy cream

3 cups Chicken Stock (see page 231)

2 large carrots, peeled and cut in half lengthwise and then into ½-inch dice or
*   into quarters lengthwise and then into 3-inch sticks*

1 medium zucchini, cut into ¾-inch dice or into quarters lengthwise and then
*   into 3-inch sticks*

1 cup frozen peas

Salt and pepper to taste

¼ cup chopped fresh parsley

Prepare the omelet: In a medium omelet pan, melt the butter. In a bowl, whisk together the eggs, water, salt, pepper. Stir in the herbs and cheese. Pour into a nonstick pan, and cook over low heat, loosening the sides gently as it cooks. When the omelet is about two-thirds cooked, slide it out onto a plate; then, holding the plate by its rim, turn it upside down, and let the omelet fall gently back into the pan, cooked side up. Cook the other side until done, then remove from heat and set aside.

Now prepare the mushroom mixture: In a large, deep sauté pan, heat the olive oil over high heat. When the oil is hot, add the mushrooms, and sauté until they start to brown, stirring constantly. Add the red pepper flakes, prosciutto, salt, pepper, and garlic, and sauté for 2 to 3 minutes. Carefully add the brandy, bring to a boil, and continue cooking to reduce to a glaze. The liquid should be almost gone, the mushrooms should be well coated. Remove from heat and set aside.

On to the turkey: Remove the skin and discard. Place the breasts top side (where the skin was) down on a flat surface. Remove tenderloins (you may freeze or otherwise save for another use). Butterfly each breast so that it looks like an open book. Cover with plastic film or waxed paper and pound, in down and out motions, to ¼-inch thickness, or slightly thicker.

Cut the omelet into 1-inch-wide strips and lay the pieces across the middle of each pounded turkey breast (that is, across the width of each "open book" from left to right). Sprinkle with the salt and pepper, and pour the mushroom mixture on top. Do not overpour. If there is any left over, reserve for later.

Roll each turkey breast like a log. Starting with the edge nearer you, fold the outer edges in (as you would a tortilla) and continue rolling, tucking and tightening as you go. Roll the edge of the meat tightly away from you. Continue rolling gently over the filling. End with turkey meeting turkey; the filling should be sealed inside. Set the rolls seam side down.

Now secure each log with kitchen twine: Gently tie a length of it around the circumference of the log at one end, and repeat every inch or so until you reach the other end. Dust each turkey roll on all sides with the seasoned flour. Brush off any excess.

In the same pan in which you sautéed the mushrooms, heat the olive oil over medium-high heat. When the oil is hot, brown the turkey rolls for about 2 minutes per side (4 turns) over high heat. If the pan is too crowded, brown each roll separately, then return them to the pan.

Deglaze with the brandy, and continue cooking to reduce to a glaze. Add the cream and stock, and bring to a boil. Reduce heat and simmer for 20 to 25 minutes, rotating the rolls every few minutes to immerse each side in the liquid. If the carrots and zucchini are cut into small dice, add for the last 5 minutes of cooking; if cut into larger pieces, add for the last 10 minutes.

After the total 20 to 25 minutes' simmering, remove the turkey rolls to a plate. Add the peas to the pan, and cook for 3 minutes. Remove the vegetables with a slotted spoon and set aside.

Continue simmering for 4 to 5 minutes, or until the sauce is thickened and coats the back of a spoon. Season to taste with salt and pepper. Add any reserved mushroom mixture to the sauce.

Remove the twine from each turkey roll, and slice into ½-to-¾-inch disks. Lay slices overlapping on a serving dish, and spoon the sauce over the turkey. Surround with the mixed cooked vegetables, sprinkle with the parsley, and serve.

Swordfish Scaloppine "Pizza Style"

SCALOPPINE DI PESCESPADA
ALLA PIZZAIOLA

SERVES 6 GENEROUSLY

This Sicilian dish takes its name from the combination of ingredients in the sauce—almost the same as used for topping pizza.

6 tablespoons olive oil

6 cloves garlic, thickly sliced

¼ teaspoon red pepper flakes

2 tablespoons chopped fresh Italian parsley

1 28-ounce can Italian-style tomatoes, drained and chopped, juice reserved

Pinch sugar (optional)

½ cup clam juice

½ teaspoon dried oregano

3 large swordfish steaks, cut at least 1 inch thick (12 to 14 ounces each)

½ teaspoon salt

¼ teaspoon freshly ground black pepper

¼ cup flour

3 eggs, beaten

1½ cups Italian-Style Bread Crumbs (see page 230)

In a saucepan, heat 3 tablespoons of the olive oil over medium-high heat. Sauté the garlic and red pepper flakes until the garlic is tender and aromatic, but not brown, about 1 minute. Stir in 1 tablespoon of the parsley. Add the tomatoes and cook, stirring well, until most of the water has evaporated, about 7 minutes. (Add the sugar if the tomatoes are tart.) Pour in the clam juice and reserved tomato juice, and add the oregano. Bring to a boil, then simmer, stirring regularly, about every 5 minutes, until the sauce is slightly thickened and has a rich aroma, about 20 minutes.

While the sauce is simmering, slice the swordfish steaks into scaloppine with a long, thin, very sharp knife: Trim away any skin and excess fat from the fish, then lay the steaks flat on a cutting board. Slice in half horizontally with long, gentle back-and-forth strokes. Press down on the fish with your free hand to maintain an even density and feel where the knife is. Separate the slices and again slice in half horizontally to obtain four 1/4-inch-thick scaloppine from each steak. Place the scaloppine between pieces of plastic wrap or waxed paper and pound gently with a flat mallet or, for thinner and flatter scaloppine, the bottom of a small, heavy pan.

Season both sides of the scaloppine with the salt and pepper. Place the flour, eggs, and bread crumbs in three separate shallow dishes. Coat each piece of swordfish in the flour, and tap gently to remove any excess. Dip both sides in the eggs and coat with bread crumbs.

In a large skillet, heat the remaining 3 tablespoons olive oil over medium-high heat. When the oil is hot, fry the scaloppine, a few at a time, in the oil until golden and tender, about 1 minute per side. Remove to a platter and cover with foil to keep warm while frying the other fish.

Pour the sauce onto a serving platter and arrange the swordfish scaloppine on top. Sprinkle with the remaining 1 tablespoon parsley and serve.

Veal Stew with Artichokes and Lemon

FRICASSEA DI VITELLO CON CARCIOFI

SERVES 6

In the latter part of the eighteenth century, it became fashionable for the Sicilian nobility to hire French chefs. They brought a distinct new character to the tables of their wealthy patrons. This recipe reflects that foreign influence, which ultimately became absorbed and reinterpreted by generations of Sicilian *monzù* (master chefs) that followed.

4 fresh artichokes (see instructions), or 1 14-ounce can whole baby artichoke hearts, rinsed, drained, and cut in half

Water to cover fresh artichoke hearts, mixed with the juice of ½ lemon

3 pounds veal stew meat (from the shoulder), trimmed and cut into 1½-to-2-inch cubes

¼ to ½ cup flour, seasoned with ½ teaspoon salt and ¼ teaspoon pepper

6 tablespoons olive oil

4 large cloves garlic, thickly sliced

½ teaspoon red pepper flakes

3 teaspoons lemon zest

1 cup chopped onion

¾ teaspoon salt

½ teaspoon plus pinch freshly ground black pepper

¾ cup white wine

3 cups Chicken Stock (see page 231)

½ cup freshly squeezed lemon juice (from 2 lemons)

2 large eggs

½ cup chopped fresh parsley

If using fresh artichokes, prepare as follows: Snap off the outer leaves until you reach the yellow-green tender inner leaves. Trim the bottom and peel the tough dark-green outer layer of the stem. Cut the artichokes in quarters. Remove the remaining leaves and fuzzy chokes with a small paring knife. Place the artichoke hearts in a glass bowl with the water and lemon juice. If using canned, prepare as instructed above.

Dust the veal with the seasoned flour. Brush off any excess flour. In a Dutch oven or large, deep sauté pan, heat 3 tablespoons of the olive oil over medium-high heat. When the oil is hot, add the veal, in batches, and brown. Do not crowd the pan. Add oil as necessary for the subsequent batches. Remove each batch when done, and set aside.

Add any remaining oil to the same pot or pan, and heat well. Add the garlic, red pepper flakes, lemon zest, onion, ½ teaspoon each of the salt and pepper, and artichoke hearts. Return the veal to the pot and stir well to mix. Add the wine, stirring well to dislodge any browned bits from the bottom of the pot. Continue cooking to reduce liquid by half, for 3 to 4 minutes. Add the stock and lemon juice and bring to a boil. Reduce heat and simmer, covered, for about 1 hour and 15 minutes.

While the stew is cooking, beat the eggs with ¼ cup of the parsley, and the remaining ¼ teaspoon salt and a pinch of pepper. Whisk well and set aside.

When the stew has finished cooking, remove the meat and artichokes to a serving dish with a slotted spoon. Bring the sauce to a boil; add the egg mixture, whisking immediately. Reduce heat and continue whisking vigorously until the sauce reduces and thickens, about 3 to 4 minutes. Be careful not to cook with the heat too high, and not to stir; if you do, you'll end up with scrambled eggs.

Remove from heat and pour the sauce over the veal, garnish with the remaining ¼ cup parsley, and serve.

Veal Tonnato

VITELLO TONNATO

SERVES 6

4 sprigs fresh parsley

3 sprigs fresh thyme

1 large bay leaf

10 peppercorns, bruised or cracked

3 to 3½ pounds veal round (from the leg), in one piece

2 carrots, peeled or scraped, cut into 3-inch pieces

3 celery stalks, ends trimmed, cut into 3-inch pieces

1 large white onion, peeled and quartered

1 teaspoon salt

GARNISH

2 small thin-skinned lemons, thinly sliced in half-moon shapes

3 small round tomatoes, cut in rosettes (see tip below) or halves

2 tablespoons drained capers

3 to 6 small gherkins

1 recipe Tonnato Sauce (see page 252)

1 recipe Rice Salad (see page 68)

Prepare the Rice Salad.

Make a bouquet garni by placing the herbs and peppercorns in a cheesecloth bag, or putting in a square of cheesecloth, gathering the corners together, and tying securely at the top with kitchen twine.

Place the veal, carrots, celery, onion, and salt in a large pot with enough water to cover contents completely. Bring to a boil, and

Here is a wonderful dish, destined to grace your dinner table at summer parties. It is easily prepared ahead, so you'll have more time to spend with family and friends. The tonnato, or "tuna-style," dish appears to have its origins in the Middle Ages, when tuna was a rarity. Chefs devised this sauce to make "mock tuna" out of whatever meat was available.

skim off any film that forms. Reduce heat, cover, and simmer for
45 minutes.

While this is cooking, prepare the Tonnato Sauce.

When the contents of the pot are done, turn off heat and let the pot sit
for 10 minutes. Remove the meat to a cutting board and let rest for
10 minutes. Slice the veal into ¼-inch slices. Lay them overlapping in a
flat oval dish. Cover the slices completely with a thin layer of the Tonnato Sauce; you should not be able to see the veal underneath. Serve
the extra sauce in a gravy boat.

To decorate the dish for a grand occasion, line the outer border with
the lemon slices. Just inside that border arrange the capers. Place the
tomato rosettes as you wish on top of the veal, and a gherkin (or two if
very small) at the base of each tomato rosette. Serve with Rice Salad on
the side.

Chef's Tip

To make a tomato rosette: With a very sharp paring knife, peel the
tomato in a single strip. Roll the strip tightly. It will unravel slightly
when placed on the dish, and make a rose shape.

My Mother's Torte

My father jumped up from the table and stomped out of the dining room, slamming the door behind him. My brother leaned over, put his hand on my shoulder and squeezed gently. He caressed the back of my head as he stood up. "I'm going to talk to him," he said. "He'll come around. Just give him time. You guys are like two bulls!"

My mother turned to me: "After all these years, you still don't know how to talk to your father, and you're just like him. He could never talk to his father either." She stood slowly and, picking up our half-eaten lunches, headed to the kitchen. I sipped my wine and, stony-faced and silent, looked out the window to the beach in the distance. A minute later she was back, with a slice of ricotta torte. She put it on the table in front of me.

That was the summer I returned to Sicily to tell my father what I'd decided to do with the rest of my life. But he couldn't understand why, after the effort and commitment we had invested into getting me the best of an American education, and the years I had spent building my career as a stockbroker, I was going to throw it all away to wash dishes in a restaurant.

Twelve years in America, and for what?" he had bellowed earlier, rising from his chair. "To work as a manual laborer . . . Great! This is what America has done for you! Where is your ambition? I should have never let you go there. Thirty-two years old, with a college degree, and he quits his job because he wants to work in a restaurant! You're killing me!" That's when he slammed the door behind him.

You know, Nicolino," my mother now said calmly, "your grandfather wasn't too keen on your father's career choices." She ran her hand across her forehead and sighed deeply. "Your grandfather had built his business from scratch, you know, piece by piece, with his own hands. He was only sixteen when his father died, and he was the provider for the family. He put his brother through school and supported his mother. He hadn't had much of an education, but that didn't stop him from building a business that gave him income, property, and a place in society. And just like your father, he sent his son away to school, to the University of Rome. That's where your father and I met. That's when everything changed."

There were no tears in my mother's eyes, yet I could see that this was summoning difficult memories.

She continued: "Your grandfather Don Nicola dreamed that one day your father would work with him. That was the tradition. It was the way things were done. It was expected of him. Your grandfather thought that once his son came back from school, he would meet a nice Sicilian girl in town, get married, have children, and live in the house Don Nicola had had built next to his.

What Don Nicola didn't know was that your father hated everything about the business and the way of life that came with working the land, managing the assets, and living in a small town. But he was almost resigned to his father's wishes when we met."

I had never heard this side of the story, and the surprise must have been written on my face, for my mother paused and laughed softly. "I wasn't exactly what your grandfather had in mind. I wasn't Sicilian, and my family was not well off. And when Don Nicola forced your father to make a choice, he chose me. For a long time they didn't speak to each other. Your father communicated through his brothers.

Your grandma had to travel to Palermo to see him because your father wouldn't go back to Alcamo.

It was a long time. It was a hard time. Your father never said much about it, but I knew he was sad. He built his own enterprise from scratch in Palermo. He was driven, like a madman. I guess he thought he had to prove something to himself, and to his father. We had even planned to immigrate to America, which, of course, would have made it even more difficult for any reconciliation.

Then you came along. And for the first time in a long time, the family was together again. These two bulls started talking to each other once more." She laughed out loud. You should have seen your grandfather around you. All the love and tenderness that he'd kept buried inside came out. But there wasn't much time left. He passed away two years later. I know that your father still wishes he could have had back some of the time he wasted being angry. There's so much he wishes he could have done. But time is the only thing you can't make more of."

She held my face with her hands and wiped the tears from my eyes. "Go to the beach, take a walk, calm down. Think about what you have to do, but don't throw your time away."

When I returned to the house later that afternoon, I found my father at the dining room table, eating a piece of ricotta torte. We were alone in the room. I poured us each a glass of Marsala and sat down across from him. *"Papà, ti voglio bene"*—I love you—I said in a whisper. "But I have to do this. I don't know where it will take me, but if I don't do it now, I will die inside."

He pushed his plate toward me. "Here, have some. I don't know how your mother does it, but hers tastes better than anyone else's."

There, at the table that had witnessed good times and bad, so much joy and passion, so many meals and hopes and dreams and disappointments shared, we

Baked Pear Half-Moons

Baked Ice Cream Pie with Strawberries

Broiled Zabaglione with Berries

Easy Chocolate Mousse

Chocolate Mousse Cannelloni

Crêpes with Ricotta

Crêpes with Banana

Aunt Buliti's Crêpes

Italian Floating Islands

My Mother's Cake

Ricotta Cake with Coffee and Chocolate

Ricotta Torte with Two Chocolates

Mixed-Berry Napoleons

Heavenly Tiramisù

Peach Tart

Chocolate Mousse Roll

Strawberries with Balsamic Vinegar and Mint

Mixed Fruit Tart

Baked Pear Half-Moons

MEZZELUNE DI PERE

SERVES 6 TO 8

6 tablespoons butter

3 cups diced pears (2 firm pears such as bosc or comice), cut in ¼-inch dice

¼ cup rum

½ cup sugar

1 cup heavy cream

2 tablespoons freshly squeezed lemon juice

2 sheets 9½ x10-inch frozen puff pastry, thawed and cut into 6 to 8
   5-inch circles

1 egg, lightly beaten

1 recipe Vanilla Cream Sauce (see page 257)

This is simple, yet eye-pleasing enough to impress your dinner guests. You don't have to reveal how easy it actually is to assemble—just sit back and enjoy the compliments.

Preheat oven to 400°.

In a large sauté pan, melt the butter until bubbling. Add the pears and cook, stirring often, until they soften and release their juice, 4 to 6 minutes. Pour on the rum and carefully light it with a long matchstick, keeping face and hands clear. It will flame up; cook until the alcohol is burned off and the flame subsides, about 1 to 2 minutes.

Remove the pan from heat and scoop out the pears with a slotted spoon, leaving as much juice in the pan as possible. Stir the sugar into the pan juice. Return the pan to heat and simmer, stirring occasionally, until the sugar turns the color of dark tea. Add the cream carefully: as soon as it touches the sugar mixture, it will start to splatter, so again keep face and hands clear; the splattering should subside after about a minute. Simmer what is now a caramel cream sauce, stirring often, until the caramel dissolves and the sauce thickens slightly, 3 to 4 minutes. Set aside.

Mix the lemon juice with the pears. Place the rounds of puff pastry flat on a counter or pastry board. Spoon about ½ cup of the pear mixture in the middle of each round. Fold the pastry over into a half-moon shape and seal the edges by pinching them together. Place the pastries on an ungreased baking sheet and brush with a thin glaze of the beaten egg. Cut one or two slits as vents in the top of each pastry. Bake for 25 to 30 minutes, or until dark golden brown.

To serve, pour Vanilla Cream Sauce into each of 6 to 8 dessert plates. Place the pastries on top, and pour the warm caramel cream sauce over them.

Baked Ice Cream Pie with Strawberries

TORTA DI GELATO AL FORNO

SERVES 6 TO 8

1 quart strawberry or vanilla ice cream
1½ cups quartered fresh strawberries or other berries
6 tablespoons cassis (optional)
4 tablespoons sugar
1 16-ounce purchased pound cake
3 egg whites
1 recipe Strawberry Sauce (see page 262)

Mothers all over the world are ingenious when it comes to pleasing their kids, and my mother was especially so. Here is one of her most successful creations. You need to start this recipe early on the day you plan to serve it—or even the day before.

As mentioned above, begin this recipe the day or morning (9 hours or more) before serving.

Take the ice cream out of the freezer and let it soften for 30 minutes, or until it can be stirred. Place the strawberries in a bowl with the cassis and 1 tablespoon of the sugar, and marinate for 30 minutes. Drain the strawberries and reserve the marinade.

Eight hours before serving, or preferably the day before, pour the softened ice cream into a large bowl and fold in the strawberries.

Line a 9x5x3½-inch loaf pan (slightly bigger is fine) with plastic wrap, leaving about 3 inches overhanging on all sides. Cut the pound cake in ¼-inch slices. Lay the slices on a baking sheet or cutting board and brush with the reserved marinade. Line the bottom and sides of the loaf pan with the slices of pound cake, pushing down to mold them to the shape of the pan. Do not worry about breaking; you can easily patch by pressing over with smaller pieces of cake. Fill the pan halfway with ice cream, and cover with a layer of cake slices. Pour in the rest of the ice cream, up to about 1 inch from the top of the pan, and cover the ice cream with another layer of cake slices. Fold the plastic wrap over the cake and place the pan in the freezer to harden.

Just before serving, preheat oven to 450°.

Beat the egg whites with an electric mixer until frothy, 1 to 2 minutes. With the mixer running, slowly add the remaining 3 tablespoons sugar and beat until the egg whites start to form stiff peaks and have a shiny gloss, 4 to 5 minutes. Transfer into a pastry bag equipped with a star tip.

Remove the cake from the freezer, unmold it onto an ovenproof serving dish, and peel off the plastic wrap. Pipe the egg white over the entire cake surface.

Bake until the meringue peaks begin to brown, about 5 to 6 minutes. Serve with Strawberry Sauce on the side.

OFFERTA DELLA SETTIMANA

FRUTTA FRESCA

Banane Chiquita	2.900
Mele Orangold	1.450
Uva di Sicilia	2.900
Pere Williams	2.150
Mele Royal Gala	1.450
Insalata	1.500
Patate Viterbo	850
Limoni di Sicilia	1.500

Broiled Zabaglione with Berries

ZABAGLIONE GRATINATO CON FRUTTA DI BOSCO

SERVES 6 GENEROUSLY

2 pounds mixed berries or soft fruit such as peeled peaches, peeled plums,
*   or cherries, pitted*
¼ cup sugar
6 egg yolks
4 tablespoons sugar
3 tablespoons orange juice
3 tablespoons Grand Marnier or Marsala

Preheat oven broiler.

Divide the berries among 6 individual gratin dishes and sprinkle evenly with half of the sugar (4 tablespoons).

Place the egg yolks, the remaining sugar, and orange juice in the top of a double boiler, and whisk constantly over simmering water until the yolks become thick and frothy, about 4 minutes. Remove the double boiler from heat and stir in the Grand Marnier. Return to heat and whisk the zabaglione again until thick and warm.

Spoon evenly over the berries and sprinkle with the remaining sugar. Bake under the preheated broiler until the top is just brown, about 1 minute. Serve immediately.

My mother found kitchen inspiration in women's magazines, and often came up with her own interpretation of the recipes that she found in them. Here is a twist on the classic zabaglione recipe; the "au gratin" effect gives a new personality to the familiar preparation.

Chef's Tip

At specialized kitchen shops you can find a small hand-held chef's blowtorch, which is ideal—and more effective than the broiler—to brown the top of this dessert. The blowtorch must, however, be handled with great care.

Easy Chocolate Mousse

MOUSSE DI CIOCCOLATO

SERVES 6

1 cup semisweet chocolate morsels (6 ounces)
3 cups heavy cream
2 tablespoons sugar
Additional heavy cream and sugar for whipping

Melt the chocolate morsels in the top of a double boiler. Whisk in 1 cup of the heavy cream until well blended. Remove from heat. Let sit for 20 to 30 minutes to come to room temperature.

In a large, chilled mixing bowl, combine the remaining 2 cups cream and the sugar. Use a hand or electric mixer to whip them together until stiff peaks form when the beaters are stopped and lifted out.

Gently fold one-third of the melted chocolate mixture into the whipped cream. Add the second third, and fold in gently. Add the last third, and fold in gently. If the mousse becomes soft, don't worry. Chill in a bowl for 15 to 20 minutes, and it will be as good as new.

Serve family style, in a big bowl, with sweet whipped cream on the side.

Chef's Tip

For a more elegant presentation, fill a pastry bag equipped with a star tip with the mousse and pipe it into individual bowls or glasses. Sprinkle with grated white or dark chocolate, and top with sweet whipped cream.

Who said you have to slave all day to prepare a good chocolate mousse? Here is the easy recipe you've been waiting for.

Chocolate Mousse Cannelloni

CANNELLONI AL CIOCCOLATO

SERVES 6

Cannelloni dishes made with pasta or crêpes are usually savory, but here's a sweet use of the term, to add to your collection of favorite desserts.

1 recipe (6) Chocolate Crêpes (see page 270)
1 recipe Easy Chocolate Mousse (see page 201)
1 recipe Vanilla Cream Sauce (see page 257)
1 recipe Chocolate Sauce (see page 260)
6 tablespoons grated dark chocolate

Prepare each of the recipes.

Place the crêpes on a flat surface. Spoon or pipe some of the mousse into the center of each crêpe. Fold the ends toward the center, overlapping to close.

With squirt bottles or spoons, make concentric circles, one of each sauce, over the center part of 6 dessert plates. Drag a knife point through the circles at 2-inch intervals to create a design. Place a rolled crêpe on top of the sauce on each plate, sprinkle with grated chocolate, and serve.

Crêpes with Ricotta

CRESPELLE RIPIENE DI RICOTTA DOLCE

SERVES 6 TO 8

1½ cups ricotta cheese
2 large eggs
4 tablespoons sugar
1¾ ounces dark chocolate, grated
½ teaspoon orange liqueur
3 to 4 oranges (only if making bundles)
1 recipe Sweet Crêpes (see page 268)
2 tablespoons sugar
1 recipe Vanilla Cream Sauce (page 257)
1 recipe Chocolate Sauce (page 260)
¼ cup toasted slivered almonds (optional; see tip below)

Preheat oven to 400°.

Mix the ricotta, eggs, sugar, chocolate, and orange liqueur together with a hand blender. Chill.

With a lemon stripper or channel knife (see tip below), cut the skin of the oranges into 10 4-to-5-inch-long strips.

Make the crêpes.

Place ¼ cup of the ricotta mixture in the center of each crêpe. If you want little bundles: Pull each up into a bundle, and tie with the orange-rind "string." If you want rolls: Fold three "corners" to the inside, then roll the entire crêpe into a fourth fold—as if you were rolling a burrito.

A little invention and a bit of passion will transform even the most mundane of dishes, Cinderella-like, into fabulous princesses. Here's the proof. (You may make these as bundles or rolls.)

Place the bundles or rolls, fold side down, on a nonstick or greased sheet pan and sprinkle with sugar. Bake for 5 to 8 minutes, or until the sugar is melted and the center mixture is warm.

Drizzle the sauces on each of 6 to 8 dessert plates (however many crêpes you've made), and place the bundle or roll on top. Sprinkle with the almonds if desired, and serve.

Chef's Tip

You can toast nuts on the stovetop in a nonstick pan. Just keep shaking the pan over medium-high heat until nuts turn brown, about 2 to 3 minutes.

Lemon strippers or channel knives can be purchased in any good cookware store. With their stainless-steel heads and one-notch blades, they produce great citrus strips.

Crêpes with Banana

CRESPELLE RIPIENE DI BANANA

SERVES 6

1 recipe Sweet Crêpes (see page 268)
1/4 cup unsalted butter
2 tablespoons light brown sugar
3 medium bananas, cut in 1/4-inch slices
1/4 cup plus 1 teaspoon (optional) rum
2 to 3 ounces dark chocolate, grated
1 cup heavy cream
1 tablespoon sugar
1 recipe Chocolate Sauce (see page 260)
Chocolate shavings

Once my mother learned to make crespelle, *there was no end to what she could do. My father got into creative competition with her, and this is one thing he came up with.*

Make the crepes and lay them on a flat surface.

Preheat oven to 400°.

In a medium sauté pan, melt the butter. Add the brown sugar, and stir with a wooden spoon over medium-high heat until the sugar is well blended. Add the bananas and cook for 2 to 3 minutes.

Add the 1/4 cup rum, and light it carefully with a long matchstick. Use common sense and extreme caution, as the flames will rise. Stand back until they die down, after about 1 minute. Once the flames have subsided, stir well. Continue to cook for 1 to 2 minutes.

With a slotted spoon, transfer an equal portion of the bananas onto one-quarter of each crêpe; sprinkle with the grated chocolate, and fold each crêpe in half and then again in half, over the filled quarter. Place the filled crêpes on a greased baking sheet, and heat for 3 to 5 minutes, or until the crêpes are warmed through.

Make the whipped cream: In the chilled bowl of an electric mixer, combine the cream and sugar, and beat until stiff peaks form. Lightly fold in the 1 teaspoon rum if desired.

Place the crêpes on individual dessert plates. Pour a few table-spoons of Chocolate Sauce over them, and top with a dollop of whipped cream. Garnish the whipped cream with chocolate shavings.

Aunt Buliti's Crêpes

CRESPELLE DELLA ZIA BULITI

SERVES 6

1 recipe Sweet Crêpes (see page 268)
½ cup plus 2 tablespoons unsalted butter
¼ cup plus 2 tablespoons sugar
3 oranges, peeled and sectioned, pith and seeds removed (see tip below)
¼ cup Grand Marnier or other orange liqueur
¼ cup freshly squeezed orange juice
1 cup heavy cream
2 teaspoons grated orange zest

Make the crêpes.

Preheat oven to 400°.

In a medium sauté pan, melt the ½ cup butter. Add the ¼ cup sugar and stir with a wooden spoon over medium-high heat until the sugar is well blended. Add the orange sections. Cook over medium heat for about 3 minutes. Add the Grand Marnier. Be careful, as it might flame up; keep face and hands clear. When flames subside, after about 1 minute, cook for another 3 minutes. Reduce heat.

With a slotted spoon, transfer the oranges (it's okay if some are broken) to the crêpes: spoon one-sixth of the cooked oranges onto one-quarter of each crêpe. Fold in half and then in half again. Place the filled crêpes on a greased baking sheet, and heat in the oven for about 5 minutes, or until heated through.

Meanwhile, add the orange juice to the sauce in the pan. Bring to a boil, reduce heat, and simmer over low heat to thicken sauce for about

Crêpes Suzette were all the rage as dessert at many restaurants in my hometown of Palermo for a long time. My aunt Buliti had her own version.

8 to 10 minutes. Turn off heat and swirl in the 2 tablespoons butter until completely melted.

Make the whipped cream: In the chilled bowl of an electric mixer, combine the cream and 2 tablespoons sugar, and beat until stiff peaks form. Fold in the orange zest. Refrigerate until ready to use.

Place the crêpes on individual dessert plates; pour a few tablespoons of the sauce over them, and top with a dollop of whipped cream.

Chef's Tip

To section an orange: With a sharp knife, slice off both ends (these will be disks). Stand the orange on one end. Following the contour, slice off the skin and white pith. Be careful not to remove the flesh. Once the flesh is exposed, hold the orange over a bowl. Insert the knife blade on one side of the skin of a segment and slice to the core. Insert the knife on the other side of the segment and let it fall into the bowl.

Italian Floating Islands

ISOLE DOLCI

SERVES 6

1 recipe Crème de Cacao and Vanilla Sauce (see page 258), chilled
1 tablespoon butter, melted
1 tablespoon plus ½ cup sugar
4 egg whites
2 ounces dark chocolate, grated, or ⅓ cup mini semisweet chocolate morsels

Make the sauce and refrigerate.

Preheat oven to 350°.

Brush the inside of 6 4-ounce ramekins with the melted butter and coat each with the 1 tablespoon sugar.

Beat the egg whites to soft peaks, gradually add the ½ cup sugar, 1 tablespoon at a time, and continue beating until the egg whites are stiff and shiny. Carefully fold in the grated chocolate. Spoon the mixture evenly into the prepared ramekins. Place these in a large baking pan half filled with hot water, and bake for 25 minutes, or until the tops are brown and crispy and the meringues cooked through.

Remove these "islands" from the oven and prick the tops with a skewer to release steam. Run a sharp knife along the inside of the ramekins and, as soon as they are cool enough to handle, carefully remove the meringues. Spoon a generous amount of the sauce onto 6 individual dessert plates, and place the meringue islands, crispy side up, on the sea of sauce.

This is a wonderfully simple yet impressive dessert. When you prepare and present this one, you'll feel like you're ready for your own cooking show.

My Mother's Cake

IL DOLCE DELLA MAMMA

SERVES 6 TO 8

If I had to choose one recipe that stands out in my mother's vast reper-toire, I'd have to choose this irresistible dessert. As with any good Genoise, this cake's flavor is even better the day after you make it. The cake "marinates," absorb-ing the rum and the cassis in the Straw-berry Sauce.

1 recipe Genoise (see page 265)
4 tablespoons dark rum
1 recipe Strawberry Sauce (see page 262)
½ recipe Vanilla Custard (see page 259)
1 recipe Chocolate and Espresso Frosting (see page 261)

Make the Genoise. When it has cooled, cut it horizontally into two layers.

Brush one side of each layer with the rum. Brush a layer of Strawberry Sauce over the rum on one layer. This will be the bottom layer of the cake. Let the Strawberry Sauce soak in for 10 minutes, and then brush on another layer.

On that layer spread a layer of Vanilla Custard. Refrigerate for 20 min-utes. Place the second layer of the cake over the custard. Transfer the cake to a cake plate.

Spread the frosting over the cake. If it is too thick, place it in a bowl in warm water for a few minutes, until it becomes pourable again.

Chill the cake for at least an hour before serving. To serve, ladle a pool of Strawberry Sauce on the dessert plates, and top with a slice of cake.

Ricotta Cake with Coffee and Chocolate

TORTINO AL CAFFÈ E CIOCCOLATO

SERVES 8 TO 10

1 cup graham cracker crumbs
2 tablespoons butter, melted
2 tablespoons plus ½ cup sugar
2 pounds ricotta cheese, drained of excess liquid
4 eggs, separated
½ cup heavy cream
¼ cup espresso or extra-strong coffee, cooled
¼ cup coffee liqueur
1 teaspoon finely grated lemon zest
½ teaspoon salt
1 cup semisweet chocolate morsels (6 ounces)

There is no end to what a Sicilian chef can do with ricotta, and here is another example—easy to make and full of flavor. This is to be made a day before serving, or early on the day you plan to serve it.

Preheat oven to 325°.

Make a graham cracker crust by mixing together the crumbs, butter, and 2 tablespoons sugar. Press the mixture into the bottom of a 9-inch springform pan.

Mix together the ricotta, ½ cup sugar, egg yolks, cream, espresso, coffee liqueur, lemon zest, and salt until creamy. In a separate bowl, beat the egg whites until they form stiff peaks. Carefully fold the egg whites into the ricotta mixture. Stir in the chocolate morsels and pour onto the prepared crumb crust.

Bake the cake for 1 hour and 15 minutes, or until just set in the middle. The cake may still seem wobbly, but should be lightly browned and cracked around the edges. Remove the pan from the oven and cool on a rack for 30 minutes. Refrigerate for at least 6 hours—even overnight—before running a sharp knife around the edge of the cake and removing from the pan. Cut into wedges to serve.

Ricotta Torte with Two Chocolates

TORTA DI RICOTTA AI DUE CIOCCOLATI

SERVES 6 TO 8

½ recipe Creamy Short Pastry (1 8-to-9-inch shell; see page 263),
    unbaked and unchilled
2 cups ricotta cheese
2 eggs
2 tablespoons sugar
¼ teaspoon orange liqueur
¼ cup chopped almonds
1¾ ounces dark chocolate, grated
1¾ ounces white chocolate, grated
Zest of 1 orange

Sometimes in life we need a little bit of sweet to smooth the rougher passages, and this little bit of sweet worked miracles for my father and me.

Preheat oven to 375°.

Make the Creamy Short Pastry.

Prepare the filling: Mix the ricotta, eggs, sugar, and liqueur. Fold in the chopped almonds, grated chocolates, and orange zest. Pour into the pastry shell. Make a lattice crust on top with any scrap dough (see tip below).

Bake until crust is golden brown, about 35 to 40 minutes.

Chef's Tip

When making the pastry shell, save any dough scraps for a lattice top. Roll the scraps together into a ball, then roll out into a rectangular shape. With a sharp knife, cut horizontal strips of the same length and width. Lay the dough strips across the pie from edge to edge, one vertically, the next horizontally, the next vertically, and so on, until the top of the pie is covered. Trim at the edges of the pan.

For a richer color or gloss to the lattice, brush the pastry with an egg wash, egg yolk or white mixed with a little water.

Roasted Pork Loin with Fennel, Peas, and Parmesan Sauce

My Mother's Cake

Mixed Fruit Tart

Mixed-Berry Napoleons

NAPOLEONE DI FRUTTA DI BOSCO

SERVES 6

1 9½x10-inch sheet frozen puff pastry, thawed (see instructions below)
2 cups fresh mixed berries (blueberries, raspberries, tiny strawberries, or larger
   strawberries diced to the size of the other fruit)
1 recipe Vanilla Custard (see page 259)
1 recipe Strawberry Sauce (see page 262)
2 to 3 tablespoons confectioner's sugar
6 sprigs fresh mint

It's amazing what can be done with frozen puff pastry and a bit of fruit.

Cut the pastry into 3-inch-square pieces, and bake according to the directions on the package. When the pastry is done (lightly golden), allow it to cool for a few minutes. Split each square into two layers. Since some purchased pastry does not rise as high as others, use your judgment: if the baked pastry is too low and thin to be split, leave as is, in one layer.

Fill a pastry bag with a small round or star tip with the Vanilla Custard.

Place a layer of the pastry on a flat surface. Top with a small amount of custard, enough to hold the fruit, but not so much that it falls out the sides. With your fingers assemble a bit of fruit on top of the cream, and top with a second layer of pastry. Repeat the layers of custard and fruit, and cap with a third and final piece of puff pastry—choose a golden-brown "top." Repeat for the remaining napoleons.

Drizzle equal amounts of the Strawberry Sauce on 6 dessert plates. Place a napoleon on the sauce on each of the plates, and a bit more fruit atop the napoleon. Sprinkle the confectioner's sugar through a small sieve over each napoleon, garnish with a sprig of mint, and serve.

Heavenly Tiramisù

TIRAMISÙ CELESTIALE

SERVES 8 TO 10

2 ½ cups espresso or strong coffee, cooled
½ cup coffee liqueur
2 17.6-ounce packages ladyfingers (72 cookies)
9 eggs, separated
1 ¾ cups sugar
1 ½ teaspoons vanilla
1 ½ pounds mascarpone cheese
1 cup finely chopped semisweet chocolate morsels (8 ounces)
½ cup sweet cocoa powder

Mix the coffee and liqueur in a large bowl. Dip in the ladyfingers in batches. Don't leave them in for too long; you want them to be moist on the outside but crunchy on the inside.

Beat the egg yolks with half of the sugar until the mixture is thick enough to form a long ribbon when you lift the beaters. (If you are concerned about using raw eggs, once you have beaten the yolks cook them in the top portion of a double boiler over high heat, whisking constantly, until they reach the thickness of a custard, 3 to 5 minutes. Be careful not to overcook them, or you'll end up with sweet scrambled eggs. Proceed with the recipe once they're cooked.) Add the vanilla and mascarpone, and beat for 2 to 3 minutes. Set aside.

Beat the egg whites, adding the remaining sugar a little at a time, until they form stiff peaks and have a glossy sheen, about 4 minutes. Gently fold the egg whites into the mascarpone mixture until it is all the same color. Gently fold in the chocolate.

We all have times in our lives when everything seems to be going our way. This recipe represents for me one of those times. I prepared a tiramisù for Oprah Winfrey to serve at one of her Book Club dinners. She loved it, and so did the three hundred people in her audience. So I say: Thank you, Oprah, for a wonderful moment in my life.

    You'll need to make this early on the day you intend to serve it, or the day before.

In a 9x17-inch glass baking dish, assemble the dessert: Layer the bottom of the pan with the moist ladyfingers, and top with a layer of the mascarpone mixture. Repeat with another layer of ladyfingers and a layer of the mascarpone mixture (see tip below). With a flour sifter, sprinkle a thin layer of sweet cocoa powder over the top. Refrigerate the tiramisù for at least 5 hours, or preferably overnight.

Chef's Tip

You might find there's enough of the mascarpone mixture left over to make another, smaller tiramisù. This usually never happens to me, because I'm always tasting to make sure the sugar and chocolate are right, so by the time I assemble the tiramisù in the baking dish, there's only just enough of the mixture for the one dish. Don't laugh—it may happen to you, too!

Peach Tart

CROSTATA DI PESCHE

SERVES 6

½ recipe Creamy Short Pastry (1 8-to-9-inch shell; see page 263), baked
   and cooled
1 recipe Vanilla Custard (see page 259)
1½ pounds fresh ripe peaches, peeled, pitted, and thinly sliced (see tip below)
2 tablespoons apricot jelly, warmed with 1 teaspoon hot water

Make the Creamy Short Pastry. When it has cooled, fill with the
Vanilla Custard. Refrigerate.

Place the peach slices on several layers of paper towels for 10 to 20 minutes to blot them.

Remove the pastry shell from the refrigerator. Lay the peach slices over
the custard in the shell, in a spiral starting in the center and covering
the custard. Brush the peaches with the jelly. Chill before serving.

Chef's Tip

You may substitute 2 14.5-ounce cans of sliced peaches, drained of
their syrup, for the fresh fruit. This tart can be made a day in advance.
Prepare the pastry shell and fill with the custard, and refrigerate
overnight. The next day, arrange the peaches and jelly, and chill.

My father was easy to please when it came to dessert. My mother knows how much he likes desserts made with fruit, and this is one of her hits.

Chocolate Mousse Roll

TRONCO NATALIZIO

SERVES 6

2 recipes Genoise (see page 265)
2 tablespoons confectioner's sugar
1 recipe Easy Chocolate Mousse (see page 201)
¼ cup coffee liqueur or chocolate liqueur
3 ounces slivered almonds
5 maraschino cherries, cut in half

Preheat oven to 350°.

Spray an 11x17-inch baking pan with nonstick spray, and line with a piece of parchment paper cut to fit the pan. Spray the paper with nonstick spray. Spread the Genoise batter evenly to the edges of the baking pan. Bake for 15 to 20 minutes, or until the cake is a light golden brown and springs back to the touch.

Let the cake cool completely before removing from baking pan and removing parchment paper. Trim the edges of the cake if slightly uneven, brittle, or overcooked. Cut a piece of aluminum foil larger than the cake and sprinkle with confectioner's sugar. Transfer the cake to the foil, "golden side" down.

To roll the cake: Sprinkle the exposed side of the cake with confectioner's sugar, sifted through a sieve. Lay a piece of parchment paper on top, and a clean linen kitchen towel on the parchment paper. (The towel is a place holder to help the roll take shape.) Gently roll from one end of the rectangular cake, as tightly as possible, using the aluminum foil underneath to help you. Even if small cracks appear, con-

When I was a boy, this dessert appeared in the windows of all the pastry shops in town at Christmas. My version of this popular holiday treat is a simpler version of the classic.

tinue to roll. Wrap the rolled cake carefully with plastic wrap, and refrigerate for 30 to 45 minutes.

Prepare the Easy Chocolate Mousse.

When the cake is chilled sufficiently, carefully unroll, removing towel, parchment paper, and aluminum foil. Brush the inside of the cake with the liqueur. Spread half of the Chocolate Mousse about ¼ inch thick over the rectangle, leaving a 1-inch border on each side. Carefully roll the cake up again, and place it seam side down on a serving platter. Frost with the remaining Chocolate Mousse. Decorate with the almonds and maraschino cherries. Refrigerate before serving. This cake can be made and assembled the day before serving. Indeed, its rich texture and flavors are even better the second day.

Strawberries with Balsamic Vinegar and Mint

FRAGOLE CON ACETO BALSAMICO E MENTA

SERVES 6

3 pounds fresh strawberries, hulled and quartered
4 tablespoons balsamic vinegar
5 tablespoons sugar
2 tablespoons chopped fresh mint

Place the strawberries in a large bowl, add the remaining ingredients, and stir well to incorporate the flavors. Marinate for at least 1 hour, stirring well every 20 minutes (see tip below). Serve over ice cream or by itself in a dessert cup.

Chef's Tip

The vinegar will extract juice from the strawberries, and this will mix with the sugar to create a thick syrup at the bottom of the bowl. It is therefore important to stir well every 20 minutes to ensure that the strawberries are marinating uniformly.

Sometimes all you need for dessert is fruit, with a little company. This unusual combination of ingredients will be a pleasant surprise for your guests.

Mixed Fruit Tart

CROSTATA DI FRUTTA MISTA

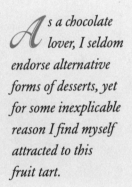

As a chocolate lover, I seldom endorse alternative forms of desserts, yet for some inexplicable reason I find myself attracted to this fruit tart.

SERVES 6

1 recipe Short Pastry (see page 267)
1 recipe Vanilla Custard (see page 259)
½ pound fresh strawberries, hulled and cut into ¼-inch slices
2 bananas, cut into ¼-inch slices
3 kiwis, peeled and cut into ¼-inch slices
¾ cup apple jelly

Preheat oven to 375°.

Make the Short Pastry, and roll out on a lightly floured surface into a 12-inch circle. Gently nudge into an 11-inch tart pan and trim off the excess. Prick here and there with a fork to prevent bubbles from forming when baking. Line the inside of the pastry shell with foil or parchment paper and fill with dry beans or rice, and bake until the edges are golden brown, 15 to 18 minutes. Carefully spoon out the beans or rice and remove the foil or parchment paper. Return the shell to the oven to brown and dry evenly, 6 to 8 minutes more. Remove and let cool.

Make the Vanilla Custard. Pour into the cooled shell and spread smooth. Carefully arrange the sliced fruit in close alternating rings on top. Heat the apple jelly so that it will spread easily, glaze the fruit, preferably with a wide pastry brush filled with plenty of glaze, in spoke pattern, dabbing from the center out to the edge of the pastry. Refill the brush as needed, and repeat until the tart is sealed and shiny with jelly. Refrigerate at least 1 hour, until set, before serving.

Mariolino
il Mariuolo

My brother, Mario, is three years younger than I, and as perhaps all younger brothers do with their older siblings, he tested the limits of my patience continuously when we were children. My parents called him Mariolino, "Little Mario," but I nicknamed him Mariuolo, which means something like "little rascal." He didn't know the meaning of this until he was given a dictionary for his ninth birthday.

Years later, after I had moved to the United States, of course I missed my family, and certainly my brother. That old saying that you don't know how much you'll miss something until you don't have it isn't just an old saying. Eventually my brother joined me in America. We were roommates in college here, and we grew closer as friends and confidants. After college, separate careers brought us both to Los Angeles where, over the years, we have grown even closer to each other as brothers.

During the rocky times after I left my job as a stockbroker to become a chef, I found myself perilously close to financial ruin. I had been trying to build my new career and get a cooking show produced. I was ready to throw in the towel, along with the chef's cap. At the lowest point of what seemed such an ill-conceived adventure, however, I found strength in my brother's support.

We had been in the habit of eating together a couple of times a week, usually on Wednesdays for lunch and on Sundays for dinner at my house. Mario loved spending time with Nanci and me, just hanging around waiting for the big meal and afterward sipping wine and smoking the occasional cigar.

After one memorable Sunday meal, as we were relaxing together, Mario pulled out a plain white envelope and, without much ceremony, handed it to me. I opened it and inside found a signed blank check and a handwritten note: "I believe in you," it said.

I never cashed that check, but I did carry it in my wallet for the longest time. It became a talisman, and a symbol of what my brother meant to me.

A few months later, just as things were starting to turn around for me, my brother announced that he was being transferred to Singapore. We continued our twice-weekly meals together, right up to the last lunch on his final day in Los Angeles. I can't recollect what we ate, but we ate and drank a lot, and laughed a lot. As always, we talked about our hopes and our ambitions, but we never mentioned that this would be our last meal together for a very long time. When I hugged him good-bye we held each other a little longer and tighter than usual. There was so much I wanted to say to him, but I knew the words wouldn't come. Images of him flashed into my mind: the baby my father brought into my room the day he was born, then the toddler with blond curly hair and a mischievous smile. And now here he was, a man just like me.

I walked Mario to his car, and I handed him a plain white envelope. No, it wasn't a blank check—that's not what my brother needed from me. I wanted to give him something of greater value. I asked him to wait until he was on the plane to open it.

My gift to my brother was the words I had not been able to say in person:

May your destiny take you over many seas of adventure.

May your vessel carry you safely on stormy waters, away from treacherous rocks.

May your sails be pushed by the winds of your ambition.

May your rudder always obey your command.

May your journeys always end in the tranquil waters of a peaceful harbor.

May your dreams become your present.

May you, one day, look back without regrets.

But as far as your journeys take you, know that there will always be a home you can return to, a family that will welcome you, a sanctuary for your tired body and for your restless soul.

There will be a place at my table and in my heart that will forever be your own.

I love you,
Nicola

Basics

Italian-Style Bread Crumbs
Chicken Stock
Beef Stock
Tomato Sauce
Creamed Tomato Sauce
Spicy Tomato Sauce
Sea Breeze Tomato Sauce
Meat Sauce
Pizza Sauce
Parmesan Béchamel Sauce
Parmesan Cheese Sauce
Pea Sauce
Green Sauce
Mushroom Sauce
Lobster Sauce
Tonnato Sauce
Roasted Garlic Sauce
Mustard Vinaigrette

Homemade Mayonnaise
Roasted Garlic and Sun-Dried
Tomato Mayonnaise
Vanilla Cream Sauce
Crème de Cacao and Vanilla Sauce
Vanilla Custard
Chocolate Sauce
Chocolate and Espresso Frosting
Strawberry Sauce
Creamy Short Pastry
Genoise (Butter Sponge Cake)
Short Pastry
Sweet Crêpes
Chocolate Crêpes
Savory Crêpes

Italian-Style Bread Crumbs

PANE GRATTUGIATO

MAKES 1½ CUPS

½ teaspoon olive oil
1 cup plain bread crumbs
1 tablespoon finely chopped fresh basil, or 1 teaspoon dried
1 tablespoon finely chopped fresh Italian parsley
⅛ teaspoon salt
⅛ teaspoon freshly ground black pepper
2 tablespoons freshly grated Romano or Parmesan cheese

In a nonstick sauté pan, heat the olive oil over medium heat for 1 minute. Add the bread crumbs and cook, stirring, until brown, about 2 minutes.

Transfer to a bowl, add the remaining ingredients, and mix well. Store in an airtight container or self-sealing plastic bag. Bread crumbs can be frozen for up to 2 months.

Chicken Stock

BRODO DI POLLO

MAKES 2¼ QUARTS

3 to 3½ pounds chicken, cut in pieces
3 medium carrots, peeled and quartered
3 celery stalks, quartered
2 medium white onions, peeled and quartered
2 tablespoons chopped fresh rosemary, or 1½ teaspoons dried
1½ teaspoons dried thyme
2 tablespoons chopped fresh basil, or 1½ teaspoons dried
2 tablespoons chopped fresh parsley, or 1½ teaspoons dried
1¼ tablespoons whole black peppercorns
¾ tablespoon salt
1½ cups white wine
3½ cups water
3 egg yolks, beaten
3 egg whites

Homemade stock is an overnight affair, but the time and effort required will be rewarded whenever you taste a recipe that calls for it.

Place all the ingredients except the egg whites (keep these, covered, in the refrigerator) in a large stockpot. Bring to a boil, then simmer for 2½ hours, skimming the foam from the top every 30 minutes.

After the 2½ hours, turn off heat and remove the chicken; reserve for other use (see tip below). Strain the stock through a fine sieve lined with cheesecloth. Cool to room temperature and then refrigerate, uncovered, overnight.

The next day, when the fat has floated to the top and hardened, skim off and discard. Bring the stock to a boil. While it is cooking, beat the egg whites with a whisk or an electric beater until fluffy. Add to the boiling stock, reduce heat to simmer, and stir well. The egg whites will harden and entrap most of the impurities in the stock (see tip below). Strain the stock again through a fine sieve lined with cheesecloth.

The stock is ready to use now, or it may be frozen, for up to a month, for later use.

Chef's Tip

Here's an idea for the leftover chicken: Remove any bones, and chop the meat roughly. Mix well with 1 or 2 beaten eggs, and plenty of freshly grated Parmesan cheese and Italian-Style Bread Crumbs. Roll the mixture into balls. Cook for 10 to 12 minutes in the boiling stock before you add the egg whites, and serve as dumplings in your favorite soup. They can also be frozen for up to a month.

The addition of the egg whites will result in a clearer and more flavorful stock. If you don't mind a cloudy stock, you may omit this step.

Beef Stock

BRODO DI MANZO

MAKES 2¼ QUARTS

2 tablespoons flour
5 tablespoons tomato paste
6 pounds beef (or veal) bones
3 tablespoons olive oil
3 medium carrots, peeled and quartered
3 celery stalks, quartered
2 medium white onions, peeled and quartered
1¼ gallons water
2 tablespoons chopped fresh rosemary, or 1½ teaspoons dried
1½ teaspoons dried thyme
2 tablespoons chopped fresh basil, or 1½ teaspoons dried
2 tablespoons chopped fresh parsley, or 1½ teaspoons dried
1¼ tablespoons whole black peppercorns
3 dried bay leaves
4 whole cloves
¾ tablespoon salt
4 egg whites

Preheat oven to 400°.

Make a paste with the flour and tomato paste. Rub half of it over the beef bones. Mix the other half with the olive oil, and combine this mixture with the carrots, celery, and onion.

Place the bones in a large roasting pan and bake until well browned, 20 to 30 minutes, turning every 15 minutes; be careful not to burn. Place the vegetables in another roasting pan and bake on the rack below the bones for the same amount of time, turning them at the same time. Transfer the bones and the vegetables to a large stockpot (or two smaller ones if you do not have one big enough to hold the 1¼ gallons water and the bones and vegetables).

Add the water and remaining ingredients, except for the egg whites (keep these, covered, in the refrigerator), and bring to a boil. Reduce to a simmer and cook for 8 hours, skimming the foam from the top every 30 minutes. Watch the pot, and as the stock reduces add water if necessary to just cover the bones.

After the 8 hours, turn off heat and discard the bones. Strain the stock through a fine sieve lined with cheesecloth. Cool to room temperature and refrigerate, uncovered, overnight.

The next day, when the fat has floated to the top and hardened, skim off and discard. Bring the stock to a boil. While it is cooking beat the egg whites with a whisk or an electric beater until fluffy. Add to the boiling stock, reduce heat to simmer, and stir well. The egg whites will harden and entrap most of the impurities in the stock (see tip below). Strain the stock again through a fine sieve lined with cheesecloth.

The stock is ready to use now, or it may be frozen, for up to a month, for later use.

Chef's Tip

The addition of the egg whites will result in a clearer and more flavorful stock. If you don't mind a cloudy stock, you may omit this step.

Tomato Sauce

SUGO DI POMODORO

MAKES 5½ CUPS

6 tablespoons olive oil
6 whole garlic cloves, peeled
1 cup finely chopped onion
¼ teaspoon red pepper flakes
2 28-ounce cans peeled Italian tomatoes with basil, drained and chopped,
    juice reserved (see tip below)
12 fresh basil leaves, or 1¼ teaspoons dried
¼ teaspoon dried oregano
1 teaspoon salt (see tip below)

In a 3-quart saucepan, heat the oil, garlic, onion, and red pepper flakes over medium-high heat. Cook for 5 minutes, stirring well. Reduce heat to medium-low and cook for 10 minutes, stirring every 5 minutes. Add the tomatoes, basil, oregano, and salt. Stir well and cook 5 minutes over medium heat.

Add the reserved tomato juice, and bring to a boil over high heat. Reduce heat and simmer for 30 minutes, stirring occasionally.

When the sauce has finished cooking, let it cool to room temperature, and then process to a smooth consistency in a food processor. You may notice that the color changes slightly in the processor; do not worry—this is normal, and it will not affect the flavor. The sauce can be frozen for up to a month.

You can always use your favorite brand of tomato sauce in my recipes. But if you feel like some homemade magic, try this simple recipe.

Chef's Tip

This is a basic sauce used mainly to prepare other sauces. If you want to use it over pasta, you might add a bit more salt, according to your taste.

The best canned tomatoes to use here are those packed in Italy; the American product tends to be too tart. If you use American tomatoes, add ½ teaspoon sugar when you are cooking them.

Creamed Tomato Sauce

SUGO DI POMODORO AL BURRO

MAKES 2¼ CUPS

1½ cups tomato sauce, homemade (see page 235) or canned
¾ cup chicken stock, homemade (see page 231) or canned
Salt and pepper to taste
¼ cup chopped fresh parsley
3 tablespoons unsalted butter

Place the tomato sauce, stock, and 2 tablespoons of the parsley in a blender or food processor, and process to a smooth, velvety texture. Pour into a saucepan and heat. Season with salt and pepper to taste. Add the rest of the parsley. Remove from heat and add the butter, 1 tablespoon at a time, until it melts into the sauce.

Chef's Tip

For a last-minute meal, prepare the sauce with the canned tomato sauce and stock, and serve over store-bought gnocchi, ravioli, or tortellini, and be generous with the grated cheese. Who needs take-out food, with something so delicious and simple?

This is a very quick recipe, used mostly in dishes requiring an elegant presentation. It isn't just for decoration, though: the sauce has a wonderful flavor.

Spicy Tomato Sauce

SUGO PICCANTE DI POMODORO

This recipe makes enough sauce for about 2 pounds of uncooked pasta.

MAKES 2½ CUPS

1 cup tomato sauce, homemade (see page 235) or canned
1 cup chicken stock, homemade (see page 231) or canned
2 tablespoons chopped fresh parsley
4 cloves garlic, thickly sliced
⅛ teaspoon red pepper flakes
1 teaspoon cold butter

In a medium saucepan, simmer the first five ingredients until mixture reaches a saucelike consistency, 10 to 12 minutes. Puree the sauce in a blender or food processor with the butter to add a shine (see tip below, though).

Chef's Tip

If you plan to serve this sauce over pasta, do not add the butter when pureeing. Instead, after pureeing, toss the pasta and sauce together over medium-low heat for 2 to 3 minutes. Turn off heat, toss the pasta with the butter and some grated Parmesan cheese, and then watch it shine.

Sea Breeze Tomato Sauce

SUGO ALLA BREZZA MARINA

MAKES 2½ CUPS

2 tablespoons olive oil

½ cup chopped onion

4 cloves garlic, thickly sliced

1 28-ounce can Italian-style peeled tomatoes, drained and chopped,
   juice reserved

2 tablespoons chopped fresh Italian parsley

⅛ teaspoon red pepper flakes

½ cup white wine

½ cup clam juice

¼ teaspoon salt

¼ teaspoon freshly ground black pepper

The thing I miss most about Sicily is the aroma of the sea breeze in summertime. Even when I lived in the middle of the Arizona desert, I re-created a little bit of Sicily when I made this sauce.

In a saucepan, cook the olive oil, onion, garlic, tomatoes, 1 tablespoon of the parsley, and red pepper flakes over medium-high heat until most of the moisture is reduced, about 7 minutes. Pour in the wine and continue cooking until liquid is reduced by half. Add the reserved tomato juice and clam juice. Season with salt and pepper, bring to a boil, and then simmer for 6 to 8 minutes, or until mixture has a saucelike consistency. Serve with pasta or fish, garnished with the remaining 1 tablespoon parsley.

Meat Sauce

RAGÙ DI CARNE

MAKES 6 TO 7 CUPS

5 tablespoons olive oil
1 stalk celery, chopped (see tip below)
1 medium carrot, chopped (see tip below)
1 medium onion, chopped (see tip below)
6 cloves garlic, thickly sliced
¼ cup chopped fresh basil
2 tablespoons chopped fresh Italian parsley
1 tablespoon chopped fresh sage, or 1 teaspoon dried
1 dried bay leaf
¼ teaspoon red pepper flakes
½ pound ground veal
½ pound ground lamb
½ pound ground beef
2 ounces prosciutto or ham, diced
1 cup red wine
3 cups Tomato Sauce (see page 235)
½ cup tomato paste
1 cup Beef Stock or Chicken Stock (see pages 233, 231)
1 teaspoon salt
½ teaspoon freshly ground black pepper

This sauce comes from the region of Emilia-Romagna in central Italy. These days, though, versions of it can be found throughout the country.

In a large pot, heat the olive oil over medium heat. Add the celery, carrot, onion, and garlic and slowly sauté until onion is sweet and tender, 6 to 8 minutes. Stir in the herbs and red pepper flakes. Increase to medium-high heat and add the ground meat and prosciutto. Cook, stirring often, until the meats start to brown, 6 to 8 minutes. Add the wine, gently scraping the bottom of the pot to dislodge any browned bits. Continue cooking to reduce liquid by half.

Mix in the Tomato Sauce, tomato paste, stock, salt, and pepper. Bring to a boil, and then simmer, covered, for 45 minutes, stirring occasionally. For a thicker sauce, remove the lid after 30 minutes and simmer, uncovered, until rich and concentrated.

Chef's Tip

For a smoother sauce, pulse the celery, carrot, and onion in a food processor for less than a minute to a rough paste. Put this paste in the pot.

Pizza Sauce

SUGO PER LA PIZZA

MAKES 1½ CUPS

ere is a fast and simple recipe for the chef on the go. Use it on your favorite pizza dough, or on swordfish (see page 182).

1 cup Tomato Sauce (see page 235)
½ cup tomato paste
¼ teaspoon garlic salt
¼ teaspoon oregano
¾ tablespoon chopped fresh basil
1 teaspoon sugar

Place the ingredients in a food processor and process until smooth.

Parmesan Béchamel Sauce

BESCIAMELLA ALLA PARMIGIANA

MAKES 3 CUPS

3 tablespoons unsalted butter, plus 2 tablespoons (optional)
2 tablespoons all-purpose flour
2 cups whole milk
5 peppercorns, crushed
1 dried bay leaf
¼ teaspoon salt
¼ teaspoon freshly grated nutmeg
1 cup freshly grated Parmesan cheese
¼ to ½ cup very thinly sliced fresh basil
Salt and pepper to taste

Next time you want to spike your favorite leftover pasta, pour this sauce on top and then brown the pasta under the broiler.

In a medium saucepan, melt the 3 tablespoons butter. Sprinkle in the flour, and stir with a wooden spoon until well blended. Cook, stirring, for 2 to 3 minutes. This mixture should become a thin paste, or roux. Remove from heat.

In a separate medium saucepan, heat the milk, peppercorns, bay leaf, salt, and nutmeg until steaming.

Return the roux to heat. Slowly pour in the steaming milk mixture, whisking constantly to prevent lumps. Continue whisking for 3 to 6 minutes. When the mixture just begins to thicken, remove from heat and stir in the Parmesan and basil. Season with salt and pepper to taste.

If you want to make the sauce an hour or two in advance, wipe the top surface with the 2 tablespoons butter or cover with buttered waxed paper. Gently reheat before using (don't cook).

Chef's Tip

Normally a béchamel requires equal amounts of butter and flour; this is a thinner version. If you're using this for mashed potatoes, you want it relatively thin, to leave them moist and creamy.

Parmesan Cheese Sauce

SUGO ALLA PARMIGIANA

MAKES 1½ CUPS

4 cloves garlic, thickly sliced
2 ounces ham, chopped
1 cup heavy cream
½ cup Chicken Stock (see page 231)
½ cup freshly grated Parmesan cheese
¼ teaspoon salt
¼ teaspoon freshly ground black pepper

In a medium saucepan, combine the garlic, ham, cream, and stock. Bring to a boil, then simmer to a saucelike consistency for 10 to 12 minutes. Stir in the Parmesan and season with salt and pepper.

This is not meant for people counting calories. But even if you do count them, when you decide to live it up, try this sauce.

Pea Sauce

SUGO DI PISELLI

MAKES 2¼ CUPS

1 10-ounce package frozen peas (2 cups)
1 cup Chicken Stock (see page 231)
½ cup heavy cream
½ teaspoon salt
½ teaspoon freshly ground black pepper

In a medium saucepan, cook the peas, stock, and cream until the peas are tender, but still bright green, about 4 to 5 minutes. Puree in a blender or food processor. Return to the pan and season with the salt and pepper. Simmer until just thick enough to coat the back of a spoon, about 6 to 7 minutes. Set aside to cool.

Chef's Tip

When using this as a pasta sauce, add ¼ cup of freshly grated Parmesan cheese to complete the flavor. My choices of pasta for this sauce would be cheese-filled tortellini, ravioli, or gnocchi.

This is a fine alternative to the classic tomato sauce, especially on filled pasta such as cheese tortellini.

Green Sauce

SALSA VERDE

MAKES 1¾ CUPS

4 loosely packed cups fresh parsley, stems removed
¼ cup diced white onion
2 cloves garlic, peeled
4 slices day-old bread (preferably white rustic, hearty, or country),
    crusts removed
⅛ teaspoon red pepper flakes
1½ teaspoons anchovy paste
3 tablespoons freshly squeezed lemon juice
2 tablespoons white wine vinegar
⅓ cup extra-virgin olive oil
1 teaspoon grated lemon zest

Here is a wonderful sauce to serve along with your favorite meat, fish, or fowl. It's great for tasty summertime barbecue.

Place all ingredients except the olive oil and lemon zest in the bowl of a food processor. Pulse until well blended. With the motor running, add the olive oil in a thin stream to emulsify the sauce. Transfer to another bowl. Fold in the lemon zest. The sauce should be grainy, the flavor slightly tart and lemony. Refrigerate until ready to use.

Chef's Tip

If the sauce is too thick for your taste, dilute with no more than ¼ cup simmering beef stock, homemade (see page 233) or canned.

Mushroom Sauce

SALSA DI FUNGHI

MAKES 4½ CUPS

3½ cups Chicken Stock (see page 231)
¾ ounce dried porcini mushrooms
1 pound small white button mushrooms, brushed clean, cut in halves
1 pound small cremini mushrooms, brushed clean, cut in halves
5 tablespoons olive oil
8 cloves garlic, thickly sliced
1 cup white wine
¼ cup heavy cream (optional)

My passion for mushrooms is expressed in this sauce.

In a saucepan, bring the stock to a boil over high heat. Add the porcini mushrooms and stir well. Cover, turn off heat, and let the mushrooms steep for 30 to 45 minutes. Extract the porcini by straining the stock over a bowl. Set the stock aside.

Chop the porcini and mix with the other mushrooms.

In a large skillet, heat the olive oil for 3 to 5 minutes over high heat, until sizzling hot. Add the mushrooms and cook for 12 to 15 minutes, stirring every 5 minutes. Add the garlic and cook for 3 to 5 minutes, stirring well as the garlic begins to brown. Add the wine and cook for 3 minutes, stirring well to dislodge any browned bits from the bottom of the pan. Finally add the stock, and the heavy cream if desired, and bring to a boil. Reduce heat to medium and cook for 15 minutes.

Chef's Tip

This sauce can be thickened by adding a paste, or roux: Mix 1½ tablespoons softened unsalted butter and 1½ tablespoons flour. Bring the sauce back to a boil over high heat, and gradually add the roux, stirring constantly with a wire whisk. Pay close attention, because the sauce will thicken quite suddenly. You can regulate the consistency by increasing or decreasing the amount of roux you add.

Lobster Sauce

SALSA DI ARAGOSTA

MAKES 3½ CUPS

2 tablespoons olive oil
4 tablespoons butter
1 small carrot, finely chopped
1 small onion, finely chopped
1 celery stalk, finely chopped
6 cloves garlic, thickly sliced
1 dried bay leaf
½ cup brandy
Shells from 7 small steamed lobster tails, cut in 2-inch pieces
6 cups Chicken Stock (see page 231)
1 cup heavy cream

In a stockpot, heat the olive oil and butter over medium heat for 3 minutes. Add the carrot, onion, celery, garlic, and bay leaf, and cook for 10 minutes, stirring well.

Add the lobster shells and cook for 10 minutes, stirring well every 5 minutes.

Add the brandy and cook for 3 minutes, stirring well.

Add the stock and bring to a boil, then simmer, almost covered, for 1 hour. Strain the stock into a saucepan, and add the cream. Bring to a boil, and cook over medium-high heat for 30 minutes, or until the sauce is reduced to 3½ cups.

From oceans and farmlands, these finely matched ingredients give a blaze of color and great depth of flavor.

Chef's Tip

If you are storing the sauce to use the next day, let it cool to room temperature before placing in a covered container in the refrigerator.

Tonnato Sauce

SALSA TONNATA

MAKES 3½ CUPS

15 ounces canned solid white tuna packed in water, drained and flaked
1½ cups mayonnaise
2 tablespoons anchovy paste, or mashed flat anchovies packed in oil
1 tablespoon freshly squeezed lemon juice
5 tablespoons drained capers
¾ cup Chicken Stock (see page 231)

Place all the ingredients in the bowl of a food processor. Process until smooth. Refrigerate until ready to use.

*A*t some time in the Middle Ages, because of a severe shortage, tuna (tonno *in Italian) be-came even more expen-sive than meat. Legend has it that an enter-prising chef prepared this sauce to make "mock tuna" out of whatever meat was available.*

Roasted Garlic Sauce

SUGO ALL'AGLIO ARROSTITO

MAKES 2½ CUPS

2 tablespoons olive oil
½ cup chopped onion
1 tablespoon chopped fresh Italian parsley
⅛ teaspoon red pepper flakes
2 tablespoons roasted garlic pulp (see tip below)
1 cup Tomato Sauce (see page 235)
1 cup Chicken Stock (see page 231)
½ cup heavy cream
½ teaspoon salt
½ teaspoon freshly ground black pepper

This sauce is a good condiment for pasta but is even better as a dipping sauce. Try it chilled with your favorite fried finger foods, or as a twist on the traditional shrimp cocktail sauce.

In a saucepan, heat the olive oil over medium heat. Add the onion, parsley, and red pepper flakes, and sauté until the onion is sweet and tender, 6 to 8 minutes. Add the garlic pulp and mix well. Stir in the Tomato Sauce, stock, cream, salt, and pepper. Bring to a boil, then simmer until the mixture reaches a saucelike consistency, about 10 to 12 minutes.

Chef's Tip

To roast garlic: Preheat oven to 350°. Cut off the top of 3 heads of garlic to expose the cloves. Place the garlic, cut side up, in a small baking pan. Drizzle with 2 tablespoons olive oil and 2 tablespoons Chicken Stock; season with a dried bay leaf and a pinch of salt and pepper. Cover the pan with foil and bake for 45 minutes, or until the garlic is soft and sweet. Cool slightly, then squeeze the roasted garlic from the heads. For pulp, mash the softened garlic in a bowl with a spoon or fork.

Mustard Vinaigrette

VINAIGRETTE AL SENAPE

MAKES ⅜ CUP

¼ teaspoon Dijon mustard
1 teaspoon sherry wine vinegar or white wine vinegar
1 tablespoon freshly squeezed lemon juice
¼ teaspoon salt
Pinch freshly ground black pepper
¼ cup olive oil

In a small mixing bowl, whisk together the mustard, vinegar, lemon juice, salt, and pepper. Whisk in a few drops of the oil until well blended. Slowly drizzle in the remaining oil while continuing to whisk until fully emulsified. The vinaigrette will be salty and lemony.

This can also be prepared in a food processor. Combine the mustard, vinegar, lemon juice, salt, and pepper in the processor bowl, and pulse until well blended. With the motor running, slowly drizzle in the oil until the dressing is creamy and emulsified.

Homemade Mayonniase

MAIONESE CASALINGA

MAKES ¾ CUP

Yolk of 1 large egg
1 teaspoon Dijon mustard
2 teaspoons freshly squeezed lemon juice
1 teaspoon white wine vinegar
½ cup extra-virgin olive oil
Sea salt to taste

Put all ingredients except the olive oil and salt into a food processor and process until well blended. With the motor running, slowly drizzle in the olive oil and process until incorporated. Add salt to taste and blend well.

Chef's Tip

You might add paprika for a spicy finish, or roasted garlic for a different taste; see also Roasted Garlic and Sun-Dried Tomato Mayonnaise (page 256).

You can of course always buy mayonnaise at the store, but you should try this recipe at least once for a delightful taste experience.

Roasted Garlic and Sun-Dried Tomato Mayonnaise

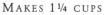

MAIONESE ALL'AGLIO ARROSTITO

MAKES 1¼ CUPS

Get ready for some spice in your life—this is not the same old dipping sauce.

1 head garlic
1 tablespoon olive oil
1 cup mayonnaise, homemade (see page 255) or prepared
¼ cup chopped sun-dried tomatoes packed in olive oil,
    drained before chopping
1 tablespoon freshly squeezed lemon juice, and more to taste
8 drops Tabasco sauce, and more to taste
1 tablespoon chopped fresh parsley

Preheat oven to 350°.

Cut off the top third of the head of garlic. Place on a piece of aluminum foil large enough to wrap the garlic. Drizzle with the olive oil. Wrap the foil around the garlic and roast for about 45 minutes, or until the garlic becomes soft. Cool.

Remove the garlic from the foil and squeeze from the outside to remove the roasted cloves, which will be soft and creamy. Discard the skin.

Place the garlic, mayonnaise, sun-dried tomatoes, lemon juice, and Tabasco in the bowl of a food processor and process until smooth. Taste, and add lemon juice and/or Tabasco if desired. Stir in the parsley. Refrigerate until ready to use.

Vanilla Cream Sauce

CREMA DI VANIGLIA

MAKES 1½ CUPS

2 egg yolks
2 tablespoons sugar
1 cup milk or half-and-half
1 teaspoon vanilla extract

Here is a simple sweet sauce to enhance your favorite pies and tortes.

Mix together the egg yolks and sugar. Scald the milk and pour in a thin stream onto the egg yolk–sugar mixture, stirring constantly. Strain into the top of a double boiler. Cook, stirring constantly, for 10 to 15 minutes, or until the sauce is thick enough to coat the back of a spoon.

Remove from heat and stir in the vanilla. Transfer to a bowl, and cover with plastic wrap on the surface to prevent a skin from forming. Refrigerate until ready to serve.

Chef's Tip

Alternatively, this sauce can be cooked in a saucepan, but remember that *gentle* cooking is the key to success for this recipe.

Crème de Cacao and Vanilla Sauce

SALSA DI CRÈME DE CACAO E VANIGLIA

MAKES 2½ CUPS

4 egg yolks
¼ cup sugar
Pinch of salt
2 cups half-and-half
2 tablespoons crème de cacao
1 teaspoon vanilla extract

Here is an interesting variation on standard vanilla sauce. You can modify it to your own taste by adding your favorite flavoring or liqueur.

In a metal bowl or the top of a double boiler, mix the egg yolks, sugar, and salt. In another pan, scald the half-and-half until small bubbles form at the edges. Carefully pour into the yolk mixture, stirring constantly. Cook over simmering water until the sauce thickens enough to coat the back of a spoon, about 15 minutes. Be careful not to boil, or the eggs will curdle. Remove from heat and stir in the crème de cacao and vanilla. Transfer to a bowl and cover with plastic wrap on the surface to prevent a skin from forming. Refrigerate until ready to serve.

Chef's Tip

Alternatively and preferably, cook the sauce in a saucepan over medium heat, stirring constantly until the custard thickens, about 8 minutes.

Vanilla Custard

BUDINO DI VANIGLIA

MAKES 2¾ CUPS

2 cups half-and-half
1 teaspoon vanilla extract
¾ cup granulated sugar
¼ cup bleached all-purpose flour
⅛ teaspoon salt
Yolks of 6 large eggs

This multi-purpose recipe works just as well as filler for fruit pies as it does as a simple pudding.

In a saucepan, heat the half-and-half over medium heat. Add the vanilla.

In a mixing bowl, stir together the sugar, flour, and salt. Whisk in the egg yolks, one at a time, until well blended. The mixture should lighten slightly in color.

Slowly, in a thin stream, pour a third of the hot half-and-half into the yolk mixture. Whisk well as you pour, to incorporate the yolks and avoid cooking them. Pour the warm yolk mixture into the saucepan with the remaining half-and-half. Whisk immediately and well. Cook over medium heat, whisking constantly, until the mixture reaches a thick, creamy consistency, about 6 to 8 minutes.

Transfer to a bowl, and cover with plastic wrap on the surface to prevent a skin from forming. Refrigerate until ready to use. The custard can be refrigerated, covered, for up to three days.

Chocolate Sauce

SALSA DI CIOCCOLATO

MAKES 1½ CUPS

½ cup heavy cream
½ cup mini semisweet chocolate morsels (6 ounces)
2 tablespoons sugar
3 tablespoons corn syrup
⅛ teaspoon salt (optional)
1 teaspoon vanilla extract

Here is your very own recipe for chocolate sauce. It's foolproof, though it has been rumored that many cooks mess it up on purpose just so they can clean the bowl— with their fingers!

In a saucepan, heat the cream, chocolate morsels, and sugar over medium-low heat until the chocolate begins to melt. Remove from heat and whisk to blend. Whisk in the corn syrup, salt if desired, and vanilla. Serve over ice cream or with another favorite dessert.

Chocolate and Espresso Frosting

CREMA AL CAFFÈ E CIOCCOLATO

MAKES 2 CUPS

6 ounces semisweet chocolate morsels
6 ounces freshly brewed or instant espresso (see tip below)
6 ounces unsalted butter, cut into small cubes

Place the chocolate morsels and espresso in the top of a double boiler over medium heat. Heat to just melting, and stir to smooth. Remove from heat, stir in butter, 2 to 3 cubes at a time, until mixture is shiny and smooth.

This frosting "sets up" as it cools. Let sit for 30 minutes, stirring occasionally, before using.

Chef's Tip

Instant espresso powder, available in many grocery stores' coffee section, is excellent for baking. You can melt the chocolate morsels and espresso in a glass bowl in the microwave for 1 minute on medium heat, then stir and add the butter as instructed above.

This frosting will go wonderfully with homemade cakes or pastries.

Strawberry Sauce

SALSA DI FRAGOLE

MAKES 1 CUP

1 10-ounce package frozen whole strawberries, partially thawed
2 tablespoons cassis
¼ cup sugar

Place the ingredients in a food processor, and pulse until pureed. (Taste. If the texture of the strawberry seeds bothers you, strain through a fine mesh or cheesecloth-lined strainer to remove them.)

This sauce can top ice cream or accompany another favorite dessert.

Creamy Short Pastry

PASTA FROLLA ALLA CREMA

MAKES 2 8-TO-9-INCH PASTRY SHELLS

3 cups unbleached white flour, plus about ½ cup extra for working the dough
½ teaspoon salt
12 tablespoons chilled unsalted butter, cut into ½-inch dice
1 egg
½ cup crème fraîche or sour cream

Crème fraîche or sour cream gives a new personality to a traditional pastry recipe.

In a food processor, combine the flour and salt with one pulse. Add the butter, and pulse until the mixture is crumbly.

In a small bowl, mix the egg and crème fraîche or sour cream. Add to the mixture in the food processor. Pulse until just moistened; the dough should look and feel very smooth.

Separate dough into two balls of equal size. On a pastry board or surface sprinkled with flour, flatten to form thick round disks. Wrap each in plastic wrap and refrigerate for 1 hour.

On a lightly floured surface, roll each disk into a thinner one with a rolling pin, starting in the center and working out from it. The disks should be slightly larger than your tart pans or pie dishes. Remove the disks to the pans, and ease in by pressing gently with your fingertips; note that you'll have to allow for shrinkage during baking. If you are using fluted tart pans, trim the crust with a paring knife. If you are using pie tins, trim the edges by working the rolling pin over the top of the pastry. Refrigerate for 30 minutes before baking and/or filling.

To prebake or "blind" bake: Preheat oven to 375°.

Prick evenly over the bottom of each pastry shell with a fork or toothpick. Line with a piece of parchment paper and fill to the brim with pie weights or uncooked dried beans (any kind will do). These weigh down the shells and allow them to hold their shape while baking.

Bake for 15 to 20 minutes, or until the crusts are a light golden brown. Remove from the oven, and remove the parchment paper and weights or beans. Bake for an additional 8 to 10 minutes to allow the bottom to crisp. Let cool completely before filling.

Chef's Tip

This dough can be frozen, wrapped in plastic and then in foil, for up to three weeks.

Genoise (Butter Sponge Cake)

IMPASTO PER IL DOLCE

MAKES 1 8-INCH ROUND CAKE, ABOUT 2 INCHES HIGH

1 cup cake flour or sifted all-purpose unbleached flour
½ cup superfine sugar
⅛ teaspoon salt
4 large eggs
1½ teaspoons vanilla extract
2 tablespoons clarified unsalted butter, reserved in a medium bowl
   (see tip below)

For this recipe, have all ingredients at room temperature, and use a free-standing mixer with a whisk attachment, or a hand mixer.

Line an 8-inch cake pan or springform pan with parchment paper, and grease and flour.

Preheat oven to 350°.

Combine the flour, ¼ cup of the sugar, and salt, and sift onto a piece of parchment paper.

In a medium bowl, beat the eggs and the remaining ¼ cup sugar on medium speed until the eggs become very light in color and the volume triples. This will take about 4 to 6 minutes with a freestanding mixer, and about 15 minutes with a hand mixer. If the eggs are beaten correctly, ribbons will form when you stop the mixer and pull up the whisk. Add the vanilla.

With a rubber spatula, gently fold the flour mixture into the egg mixture, about a third at a time, until just incorporated.

What follows is a very easy recipe for this traditional cake. The Genoise is the foundation for two recipes in this book, and more important, it can be a starting point for creating your own.

Spoon about 1 cup of the batter into the clarified butter, fold in gently, then mix back into the batter in the mixing bowl. Pour the batter into the prepared pan and place immediately in the oven.

Bake until the top of the cake is golden in color, and the sides pull away from the pan, about 20 minutes. Let cool before removing or releasing from the pan. Turn the pan over to remove the cake and the parchment paper.

Chef's Tip

To clarify butter, start with twice the amount you will need for the recipe. Melt it over low heat until the solids separate from the clear yellow liquid. Pour or spoon off the solids, and retain the liquid clarified butter. Dispose of the solids.

Short Pastry

PASTA FROLLA

MAKES AN 11-INCH PASTRY SHELL

1 ½ cups flour
½ teaspoon salt
8 tablespoons chilled butter, cut into ½-inch dice
1 egg, lightly beaten
4 tablespoons cold water

This is my version of traditional pie dough.

In a food processor, combine flour and salt with one pulse. Add the butter and pulse until the mixture is crumbly. Add the egg and water and pulse until just moistened. Turn the dough out on a flat surface and form into a ball. Flatten the ball and wrap in plastic wrap. Refrigerate for at least 15 minutes. To shape the shell, roll the chilled dough out on a lightly floured surface to a diameter about ¾ to 1 inch larger than the pan.

Sweet Crêpes

CRESPELLE DOLCI

MAKES 6 TO 8 8-INCH CRÊPES

1 cup all-purpose flour, or cake flour for slightly lighter crêpes
½ cup cold milk
½ cup very cold water
2 whole eggs
2 egg yolks
3½ tablespoons clarified unsalted butter (see tip below)
2 tablespoons orange liqueur
2 tablespoons sugar
⅛ teaspoon salt
3½ tablespoons clarified butter for cooking batter, or nonstick spray

This is a funda-mental recipe in Italian cooking, though perhaps not as well known as others. It is a versatile tool for the creative home cook.

Sift flour into a blender or mixing bowl. Add the milk, then the water, blending or whisking constantly to avoid lumps. Blend or whisk in the eggs and yolks, 3½ tablespoons clarified butter, liqueur, sugar, and salt. Refrigerate for 30 minutes.

Heat a 10-inch nonstick sauté pan over medium heat and season with 1 teaspoon of the clarified butter, or with nonstick spray.

Ladle ¼ cup of the batter into the center of the pan (less if using a smaller pan). Tilt the pan in all directions so the batter forms a thin disk. In about 30 to 45 seconds, the crêpe should be lightly browned.

Shake the pan to loosen the crêpe. Turn it over with a heat-resistant spatula, tongs, or a fork. Cook the other side until dry, and remove from pan. (See tip below.) Repeat with the rest of the batter, seasoning the pan as necessary with clarified butter or nonstick spray. Stack the cooked crêpes on top of one another to keep them warm. If you are not serving them right away, place a piece of plastic wrap or waxed paper between crêpes.

If the batter becomes thick toward the bottom of the bowl and the cooled crêpes do not have tiny lacy bubbles around the outer rim, add a teaspoon of water to the batter, mix, and continue cooking.

Chef's Tip

To clarify butter, start with twice the amount of butter you need to end up with. Melt it over low heat until the solids separate from the clear yellow liquid. Pour or spoon off the solids, and retain the liquid clarified butter. Dispose of the solids.

As with pancakes, to make sure you have a perfectly greased pan, it may be wise to make a first test crêpe, which you may then discard.

When making crêpes ahead or to freeze, stack them with plastic wrap or waxed paper in between. You may store them in a self-sealing plastic bag overnight. Finished crêpes can be frozen for several weeks when wrapped well in plastic wrap, then in foil.

Chocolate Crêpes

CRESPELLE AL CIOCCOLATO

MAKES 6 TO 8 8-INCH CRÊPES

1 cup cake flour

½ cup very cold water

½ cup cold milk

2 whole eggs

2 egg yolks

3½ tablespoons clarified unsalted butter (see tip below)

2 tablespoons sugar

⅛ teaspoon salt

2 tablespoons cocoa powder

Grated chocolate or chocolate curls for garnish

3½ tablespoons clarified butter for cooking batter, or nonstick spray

Fill these crêpes with ricotta, softened ice cream, chocolate pudding, or whatever strikes your fancy. You've just opened the door to a new world of wonderful desserts.

Sift the flour into a blender or mixing bowl. Add the milk, then the water, blending or whisking constantly to avoid lumps. Blend or whisk in the eggs and yolks, 3½ tablespoons clarified butter, sugar, and salt. Refrigerate for at least 30 minutes.

Season a 10-inch nonstick sauté pan with 1 teaspoon of the clarified butter, or with nonstick spray. Ladle a scant ¼ cup of the batter (less if using a smaller pan) into the center of the pan. Tilt the pan in all directions so the batter forms a thin disk. In about 30 to 45 seconds the crêpe should be lightly browned on the bottom.

Shake the pan to loosen the crêpe. Turn it over with a heat-resistant spatula, tongs, or a fork. Cook the other side until dry, without overbrowning, and remove from pan. (See tip below.) Repeat with the rest of the batter, seasoning the pan as necessary with more clarified butter or nonstick spray. Stack the cooked crêpes on top of one another to keep them warm. If you are not serving them right away, place a piece of plastic wrap or waxed paper between crêpes.

If the batter becomes thick toward the bottom of the bowl and the cooked crêpes do not have tiny lacy bubbles around the outer rim, add a teaspoon of water to the batter, mix, and continue to cook.

Chef's Tip

To clarify butter, melt it over low heat until the solids separate from the clear yellow liquid. Pour or spoon off the solids, and retain the liquid clarified butter. Dispose of the solids.

As with pancakes, to make sure you have a perfectly greased pan, it may be wise to make a first test crêpe, which you may then discard.

Savory Crêpes

CRESPELLE CONDITE

MAKES 14 TO 16 8-INCH CRÊPES

1 cup all-purpose flour
1 cup cold water
½ cup cold milk
2 eggs
3 tablespoons butter, melted
¼ teaspoon salt
2 tablespoons olive oil

This version of crespelle *batter is solely for making savory dishes; do not use it for desserts.*

Measure flour, ¾ cup water, milk, eggs, butter, and salt into a blender or mixing bowl. Blend or whisk until smooth. Refrigerate, covered, for 15 to 30 minutes. When ready to cook the crêpes, add the remaining cold water to thin the batter to the consistency of heavy cream.

Heat a very well seasoned skillet or a 10-inch nonstick fry pan over medium-high heat and add a few drops of olive oil. Lift the pan from the heat and ladle about ¼ cup of the batter into the center. Quickly tilt the pan in all directions so the batter forms a thin, lacy pancake. Cook the crêpe for 30 to 40 seconds, until the edges curl and brown slightly. Flip the crêpe with a flexible heat-resistant spatula or nimble fingers, and cook the other side for about 15 seconds, until spotted with brown and dry. Remove from the pan. Stack the cooked crêpes on top of each other to keep them warm. (See tip below on storage.)

If the batter becomes thick toward the bottom of the bowl and the cooked crêpes do not have tiny lacy bubbles around the outside rim, add a teaspoon of water to the batter, mix, and continue cooking.

Chef's Tip

When making crêpes ahead or to freeze, stack them with plastic wrap or paper towels in between. You may store them in a self-sealing plastic bag overnight. Finished crêpes can be frozen for several weeks when wrapped well in plastic wrap, then in foil.

$\mathcal{M}$ mamma, what are you making for dinner tonight?" When I was a boy, this was the first thing I said almost every morning when I sat down to breakfast.

"Chicken," my mother might answer, rolling her eyes and waiting for the questions that would inevitably follow.

"Are you going to roast it?" my father would ask between sips of espresso.

"Why? Do you want it roasted?" My mother's displeasure with the morning ritual would start to show.

"Arrosto, Mamma, arrosto, sì! Con le patate!"–Roasted, Mamma, yes! With potatoes!–my brother would exclaim. Mario didn't always pick up on the meaning in my mother's tone of voice. Or maybe he did, but knew he would get away with his badgering.

As gourmet-chef-in-the-making, I couldn't resist throwing in my two cents' worth. "Are you going to put the spices under the skin or just sprinkle them on top, like Nonna Maria does?"

My mother would smile and ruffle my hair. My father would try to hold back his laughter, but the newspaper he held would shake up and down, betraying him.

"Nicolino," she would tell me, "today I will show you a new kind of roasted chicken. I marinated it last night with the vinegar your father brought me from Modena. Don't worry, there's plenty of garlic and rosemary. I'll roast it in the oven with the potatoes. And I'll make a cake for dessert. What would you like for pasta?"

"Spasketti!" That was Mario for you.

"Nicolino, do you want to help me make the sauce?"

"Sì, Mamma!" I would respond proudly.

As I said, my mother faced this inquisition almost every day of our lives together. Yet where others would have faltered under the pressure—of answering questions *and* satisfying appetites—she rose to the occasion, every single time. Every dinner was an event, an opportunity to top her previous exploits. Not all her culinary experiments were resounding successes. Yet my father, my brother, and I were inspired by her indomitable spirit, a spirit I have tried to conjure in the recipes collected here.

In every household, from Palermo to Pasadena and beyond, "What's for dinner?" is a daily refrain. And in every household, there's someone who'd like to please everyone with a delicious answer from the kitchen. But no matter how much we love our family, at times the thought of coming up with one more meal is just too much: we can be easily tempted to go to the phone and order pizza or Chinese take-out. Still, there's nothing that compares with a wholesome home-cooked dinner.

If you are familiar with my previous cookbooks, you know that most of my recipes are fairly simple and quick to prepare. In that regard, this collection is no different. Even though I offer some recipes for special occasions when you can and want to spend a little more time in the kitchen, most of the dishes can be made and served every day. This collection does differ from the others in one area: here I offer something in response to the many requests I've received over the years for menus.

It's not difficult to select one dish, say, a main course or a pasta, but putting an entire meal together is more of a challenge for some people. So I have taken the liberty of preparing a few menus, for every day and for special occasions. In Italy, as an old friend of mine once said, there are no rules—only suggestions. These are just that—not rules, but suggestions, which I hope will be useful and encourage your own culinary creativity. When you let your heart and passion be your guides, you can never go wrong.

The Menus

Comfort Food for Everyday Dining ✦

The following menus have been designed for everyday dining and casual entertaining. Most of them are updated versions of the rustic dishes I enjoyed at home in Sicily. The combination of flavors is bold, and the results are soul-satisfying.

This is a perfect lunch, hearty and delicious.

✦ *Stuffed Peppers with Tomatoes, Mozzarella, Capers, and Olives (page 22)*
✦ *Potato Soup with Mortadella and Salami (page 58)*
✦ *Mixed Fruit Tart (page 222)*

The appetizer here is easy to prepare, and will make your guests think they're dining in Italy. The pasta is also quick and simple.

✦ *Toasted Bread with Onion and Pancetta (page 9)*
✦ *Pasta with Sausage and Mushrooms (page 120)*
✦ *Easy Chocolate Mousse (page 201)*

This combination is a nice departure from standard fare.

✦ *Raw Mushroom Salad (page 64)*
✦ *Sausages and Peppers Country Style, with Grandma's Polenta (page 165, 77)*
✦ *Mixed Fruit Tart (page 222)*

Start with a small pasta serving, traditional in Italy, and finish with a simple yet elegant dessert.

  ❧ *Pasta with Lentils and Pancetta (page 106)*
  ❧ *Chicken Cutlets Milanese Style, with Sautéed Mushrooms,*
    Green Beans, Tomatoes, and Prosciutto (pages 148, 74)
  ❧ *Broiled Zabaglione with Berries (page 199)*

You can serve this to family and friends with pride.

  ❧ *Corn, Zucchini, and Pepper Soup (page 50)*
  ❧ *Chicken Scaloppine with Sun-Dried Tomatoes and Peas*
    (page 151)
  ❧ *Baked Pear Half-Moons (page 195)*

This menu features real comfort foods—potatoes and chocolate—and a surprising opener.

  ❧ *Baked Eggs with Spinach and Ricotta (page 11)*
  ❧ *Chicken Scaloppine with Roasted Red Pepper Sauce,*
    with Mashed Potatoes Parmesan (pages 145, 76)
  ❧ *Easy Chocolate Mousse (page 201)*

The appetizer can be prepared ahead and reheated quickly. Everyone will love the dessert, which is almost as easy to make as store-bought, but twice as tasty.

  ❧ *Braised Artichokes (page 15)*
  ❧ *Pasta with Salami and Rosemary Sauce (page 116)*
  ❧ *Chocolate Mousse Cannelloni (page 202)*

Calamari may not be to everyone's taste, but this delicious version will gain some converts. And they'll certainly eat everything on their plates in anticipation of the classic dessert.

✺ *Stuffed Calamari (page 39)*
✺ *Pasta with Shrimp and Artichokes (page 122)*
✺ *Ricotta Cake with Coffee and Chocolate (page 211)*

Dazzle your friends and family with the unusual, exotic-looking first course in this menu.

✺ *Pasta with Black Squid Sauce (page 124)*
✺ *Stuffed Cabbage Leaves Country Style (page 175)*
✺ *Peach Tart (page 218)*

Dining al Fresco ✺

When rough winter had passed, and spring was gently edging into summer, my family and I took every possible opportunity for enjoying our meals outdoors. Everything seems to taste better when you eat outside. In America, eating outdoors more often than not means a burger or hot dog on the grill. But you can enjoy a full range of meals al fresco, without a drop of barbecue sauce in sight. And you don't have to travel long distances to enjoy the experience: sometimes the perfect place is right outside your kitchen door.

The varied flavors and colors in this menu will please your guests wherever you decide to set your table.

✺ *Pasta with Swordfish, Lemon, and Capers (page 129)*
✺ *Chicken Scaloppine with Mushroom Sauce, with Sautéed Mushrooms, Green Beans, Tomatoes, and Prosciutto (pages 143, 74)*
✺ *Strawberries with Balsamic Vinegar and Mint (page 221)*

These dishes can be easily prepared ahead and transported. But be careful not to let the ice cream melt!

    Shrimp and Cannellini Salad (page 66)
      Rollatini (page 24)
        Veal Tonnato, with Rice Salad (pages 186, 68)
          Ice cream with Strawberry Sauce (page 262)

This assemblage is perfect for a big crowd. And you'll satisfy even the most die-hard barbecue fans.

    Little Bruschette (page 17)
      Sicilian Barbecue (page 171)
        Broiled Marinated Shrimp (page 169)
          Roasted Smashed Potatoes with Peppers (page 71)
            Stewed Peas with Sun-Dried Tomatoes (page 73)
            Sautéed Lima Beans (page 70)
              Heavenly Tiramisù (page 216)
                Strawberries with Balsamic Vinegar and Mint
                (page 221)

Here's a simple yet unusual gathering of flavors. This menu is great for a quick backyard meal.

    Raw Mushroom Salad (page 64)
      Pasta with Curry Sauce (page 100)
        Broiled Zabaglione with Berries (page 199)

For a lunch or dinner on the patio, try this:

    Trio of Stuffed Eggs (page 34)
      Raw Mushroom Salad (page 64)

     ❧ *Pasta with Peas and Tuna (page 110)*
       ❧ *Ice cream with Chocolate Sauce (page 260)*

The hearty appetizer and classic main dish will have everyone asking for more.

    ❧ *Pasta with Prosciutto, Spinach, and Garbanzo Beans*
       (page 112)
     ❧*Roasted Chicken with Balsamic Vinegar and Herbs*
       (page 158)
      ❧ *Mixed Fruit Tart (page 222)*

This sophisticated menu is perfect for entertaining your best friends.

    ❧ *Pasta with Fennel Sauce (page 102)*
     ❧ *Shrimp with Spicy Tomato Sauce, with Saffroned Rice*
       Timbales (pages 167, 79)
      ❧*Ice cream with Chocolate Sauce and Strawberry Sauce*
       (pages 260, 262)

Romantic Menus ❧

When life gets frantic and you're trying to do too many things at once, you may not pay enough attention to that special someone in your life. It's important to keep the flame that brought you together glowing, or to rekindle it. The following menus have been designed to help you create a romantic dining experience, just for the two of you. Take out the fine china, light the candles, arrange some fresh flowers, put soothing music on in the background, and you've set the mood for romance.

You won't have to spend all your time in the kitchen to make this meal. And as long as you *both* enjoy the pasta with garlic, no problem.

꩜ *Pasta with Garlic and Zucchini Sauce (page 104)*
꩜ *Sole Fillets with Capers and Lemon Sauce, with Saffroned*
Rice Timbales (pages 173, 79)
꩜ *Ricotta Cake with Coffee and Chocolate (page 211)*

The soup is a spectacular start to a simple, elegant meal.

꩜ *Mussel Soup with Curry (page 56)*
꩜ *Baked Tuna with Tomato Pesto (page 137)*
꩜ *Peach Tart (page 218)*

The two of you can spend time in the kitchen together making this delicious combination.

꩜ *Scallops on a Bed of Leeks and Artichokes (page 28)*
꩜ *Braised Sea Bass with Peppers and Olives (page 141)*
꩜ *Crêpes with Banana (page 205)*

Quick, easy, and bursting with flavors, this colorful meal will have you both swooning.

꩜ *Little Bruschette (page 17)*
꩜ *Salmon Scaloppine with Vodka and Caper Sauce, with*
Sautéed Spinach (pages 163, 78)
꩜ *Aunt Buliti's Crêpes (page 207)*

Here's a mix of the refined and the simple.

꩜ *Pasta with Gorgonzola and Walnut Sauce (page 114)*
꩜ *Swordfish Scaloppine "Pizza Style," with Sautéed Lima*
Beans (pages 182, 70)
꩜ *Mixed Fruit Tart (page 222)*

The colors in this array—red, white, and green—remind me of home, the most romantic country in the world.

    Green Salad with Broiled Goat Cheese (page 60)
Chicken Scaloppine with Mushroom Sauce, with Stewed Peas with Sun-Dried Tomatoes (pages 143, 73)
Strawberries with Balsamic Vinegar and Mint (page 221)

Entertaining: Parties and Gatherings

These menus have been designed with entertaining in mind. I think of them as blueprints for celebration: they are versatile and offer a range of choices, whether you're planning an elegant dinner, a casual party, or a family celebration.

Here is a wide array of choices to make a festive buffet.

    Little Bruschette (page 17)
Shrimp Fritters with Roasted Garlic Sauce (page 18)
Little Pizzas (page 20)
Rollatini (page 24)
Trio of Stuffed Eggs (page 34)
Truffled Breadsticks (page 41)
Lobster Salad (page 62)
Raw Mushroom Salad (page 64)
Rice Salad (page 68)
Veal Tonnato (page 186)
Baked Ice Cream Pie with Strawberries (page 197)

This elegant dinner will impress your most discerning guests, and it's a lot easier to put together than you'd imagine.

    Lobster Salad (page 62)
     Spinach Cannelloni (page 90)
      Chocolate Mousse Roll (page 219)

A casual and comforting meal like this is ideal for a relaxed evening with family or friends.

    Baked Zucchini Stuffed with Salami (page 13)
     Don Vincenzo's Rice and Lobster Timbale (page 93)
      My Mother's Cake (page 210)

The hearty home-style stew at the center of this meal has a special heritage. It will make your guests feel as important as the wealthy Sicilian nobles for whom an original version was once prepared.

    Crêpe Lasagna (page 92)
     Veal Stew with Artichokes and Lemon (page 184)
      Baked Ice Cream Pie with Strawberries (page 197)

With its refined simplicity, this menu will surprise even the most sophisticated gourmets.

    Little Bruschette (page 17)
     Scallops with Prosciutto and Morels (page 30)
      Baked Pasta with Four Cheeses (page 87)
       Mixed-Berry Napoleons (page 215)

Make your dining room an Italian country trattoria with this hearty combination.

❧ Little Pizzas (page 20)
❧ Sautéed Calamari with Sun-Dried Tomatoes (page 26)
❧ Crêpe Lasagna (page 92)
❧ Green Salad with Broiled Goat Cheese (page 60)
❧ Baked Pear Half-Moons (page 195)

This dinner was prepared to celebrate the Oprah's Book Club selection of Wally Lamb's novel *This Much I Know Is True*. While I am proud of every recipe, it was the tiramisù that garnered the highest praise from Oprah and her guests.

❧ Scallops on a Bed of Leeks and Artichokes (page 28)
❧ Pasta with Chicken, Sun-Dried Tomatoes, and Pine Nuts (page 127)
❧ Green Salad with Broiled Goat Cheese (page 60)
❧ Heavenly Tiramisù (page 216)

If you are looking for an unusual Thanksgiving feast, here's one that provides all the essentials of an old-fashioned American holiday dinner with a few continental twists.

❧ Pasta with Sausage and Pumpkin Sauce (page 118)
❧ Stuffed Turkey Breast (page 178)
❧ Mashed Potatoes Parmesan (page 76)
❧ Ricotta Torte with Two Chocolates (page 213)

Family Style ❧

The following menus are versions of the one-pot meals that my family enjoyed when I was growing up. The dishes are informal, easy, and comforting; they'll become favorites with your family too. Serve them family style, passed around the table from person to per-

son. Something as simple as the anticipation of a serving dish, or the spooning of glistening sauce over mashed potatoes, may well be an unforgettable moment.

Hearty, traditional comfort foods will warm the bodies and souls of every member of your family.

    Minestrone (page 54)
      Lamb Stew with Tomatoes, Garlic, and Rosemary,
          with Roasted Smashed Potatoes with Red Peppers
          (pages 153, 71)
      Aunt Buliti's Crêpes (page 207)

With their subtle flavors and light textures, these dishes are ideal for a family lunch or midweek supper.

    Braised Artichokes (page 15)
      Fragrant Chicken Soup with Meatballs (page 52)
      Crêpes with Ricotta (page 203)

This menu, perfect for a cold winter evening, starts with a luscious pasta and finishes with an equally warming sweet.

    Pasta with Cauliflower and Garlic (page 98)
      Boiled Beef Piedmontese Style (page 139)
      Ricotta Cake with Coffee and Chocolate (page 211)

This meal might seem to have many non-Italian elements. But the soup and main dish are classic Sicilian.

    Cabbage Soup (page 49)
      Roasted Pork Loin with Fennel, Peas, and Parmesan Sauce
          (page 161)
      Chocolate Mousse Cannelloni (page 202)

Each of the recipes in this menu features elements that have been "borrowed" and reinterpreted by Italian chefs over the years.

> *Fried Shrimp with Pine Nuts and Herbs (page 32)*
> *Veal Stew with Artichokes and Lemon (page 184)*
> *Mixed-Berry Napoleons (page 215)*

The focus of this rich and robust meal is the braciole, a favorite of many Italians.

> *Mushroom and Crêpe Torte (page 37)*
> *Braciole, with Sautéed Lima Beans (pages 155, 70)*
> *Ricotta Torte with Two Chocolates (page 213)*

Welcome to dinner at Grandma's house. This pleasant collection epitomizes comfort food.

> *Minestrone (page 54)*
> *Roasted Pork Loin with Fennel, Peas, and Parmesan Sauce (page 161)*
> *Italian Floating Islands (page 209)*

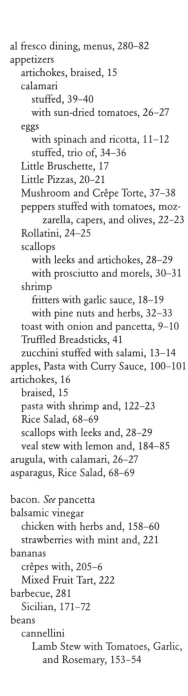